YOUR MOM'S GONNA *Love* ME

YOUR MOM'S
GONNA *Love*
ME

MATT RIFE

GALLERY BOOKS

New York   London   Toronto   Sydney   New Delhi

Gallery Books
An Imprint of Simon & Schuster, LLC
1230 Avenue of the Americas
New York, NY 10020

Note: Some names and identifying characteristics have been changed.
Some dialogue has been re-created.

First Gallery Books hardcover edition December 2024

GALLERY BOOKS and colophon are registered trademarks
of Simon & Schuster, LLC

Simon & Schuster: Celebrating 100 Years of Publishing in 2024

For information about special discounts for bulk purchases,
please contact Simon & Schuster Special Sales at 1-866-506-1949
or business@simonandschuster.com.

The Simon & Schuster Speakers Bureau can bring authors
to your live event. For more information or to book an event,
contact the Simon & Schuster Speakers Bureau at 1-866-248-3049
or visit our website at www.simonspeakers.com.

Interior design by Jaime Putorti

Manufactured in the United States of America

10 9 8 7 6 5 4 3 2 1

Library of Congress Cataloging-in-Publication Data is available.

ISBN 978-1-6680-6041-4
ISBN 978-1-6680-6043-8 (ebook)

For Papaw, who was always there for me

and gave me the life he deserved

INTRO

NEVER SAY NEVER

I lost my virginity the old-fashioned, all-American way—in high school, in the back seat of a shitty little Honda, with a girl who had a Justin Bieber tramp stamp.

I was seventeen years old, weighed 115 pounds, had gelled hair so stiff it could impale you, and a voice that hadn't even cracked yet. Yeah—think "fuckboy" without an ounce of fuck. She was my very first girlfriend who I'd met on Instagram, because honestly how the hell else do you meet anyone these days, and she was a couple years older than me, because, well—we *all* have a type.

We were in the white-trash heap that is rural central Ohio, parked in her car all the way at the bottom of the long driveway that led up to my mom's house, because I didn't even have a license yet. We were lying there in that cramped little back seat in this spooning position, playing Just The Tip—don't judge, it's how most of you got here. It was very good (for me), it was very, very fast, and I don't believe I used protection. Pretty much as high school as you can possibly get.

We had just finished and she was turning over for round two—it's a marathon, not a sprint—and that's when I saw it, right there on the small of her back in that fancy, squiggly script favored by Beliebers throughout the Midwest:

Never Say Never.

Now, I really wish I could tell you that this gave me pause. That I took in the absolute profoundness of these words and stopped myself to have a little think. Like, when she chose to get this line tattooed right above her butt, was my new girlfriend trying to be clever—maybe even encouraging—to desperate adolescent horn-balls like myself? Was this an attempt at some kind of vaguely witty quasi-sexual pun? *Hey kid, you might be fugly, but shoot your shot! So to speak!* Or was she literally just like, "That's my favorite Justin Bieber song! Put it on my back like a bullseye!"

Seriously, I didn't give a shit. It was sex! I was her "Boyfriend," I wanted her "Right Here," and I knew everything would "Be Alright" . . . even though it could've led to a "Baby."

I really lucked out there.

Because the truth is that even at that age, I had no interest in being stuck in Ohio forever. In fact, I was already ready to get the hell out. I had grown up feeling like a misfit, a white kid in a mostly white town with all Black friends. My mom loved me, but she was married to a dude who spent most of his time drinking beer and smacking me around. The closest thing I had to a dad was my papaw, Grandpa Steve, who laid tile for a living and instilled me with the dark and dangerous sense of humor I have to this day.

It was that sense of humor that I was counting on to get me out. I hadn't even graduated high school—technically I never would— but I was about to leave for Los Angeles, where I barely knew a soul and where I was determined to build a career as a stand-up.

Did I have a clue what I was doing? Fuck no! If I had any idea what was in store for me, I probably would've stayed right there in that Honda, glued to that older girl's ass and pondering the intricacies of ironic tattoos for the rest of time.

Instead, I'd spend the next few years crashing on couches, riding the bus with homeless dudes who pissed in their seats, dating more than my fair share of MILFs, and toiling away in the depressing depths of comic obscurity. I'd be half a step away from joining the army or starting a promising career as a bag boy at Ralphs. Until suddenly a single viral video would find me a global audience of millions, changing my entire life in one night—and two crazy years.

Oh yeah—did I mention I'm only twenty-nine years old? Like, right now. But I promise I read at a forty-year-old level.

Lying in that car at the bottom of that driveway in Ohio, I had no idea what the next ten years would bring. I had no idea if I'd succeed beyond my wildest dreams or fail miserably—or maybe do a little of both. All I knew was that I had nothing to lose by trying.

Never Say Never?

You're goddamn right, Justin Bieber. Never pull out of your dreams.

YOUR MOM'S GONNA *Love* ME

1

LITTLE KIDS AND CIGARETTES

Come on, Mom—just roll it down a little, all right? I can barely breathe!"

We were driving in my mom's GMC Jimmy. This truck was so old and busted I'm pretty sure my stepdad went to the used-car dealer and asked for something "in gray and rust."

She was giving me a ride to school, which didn't happen often, but I was about to run out of air because she was smoking Marlboro Lights—which happened *all the damn time*. I mean, she did a couple packs a day, at least. And of course my window was broken. It wouldn't budge.

I had my first hotbox before my first lunch box.

My mom was this tiny little blond lady, like five foot two— how on earth could her lungs churn out this much smoke? I was hacking, my throat was all scratchy, and I had my shirt pulled up over my face like a white-trash oxygen mask. I probably sounded like Darth Vader on Auto-Tune, except, you know, with a twelve-year-old's squeaky hormonal voice. And this was one of my good shirts I was stretching out! Well, as good as all my other ones, anyway. Old leftovers from Kmart with really witty slogans like "Will Trade Girlfriend for Video Games." Perfect for *not* getting a girlfriend when you're in the seventh grade.

I was small, I was skinny, I was a year younger than everyone else in my class because my mom had started me in preschool a year early, and I was convinced my teeth were way too small for my mouth—they had all these gaps between them, in the front and the sides and everywhere. With teeth that bad, living in Ohio, I very easily could've been named METHew.

Oh, and for all y'all kids out there lucky enough to be born after Kmart went out of business, it was like Walmart, except poor. A real joy to shop in.

"Mom, please—!"

"What?" she said, finally turning down the music and looking in my direction. "You say something?"

To be fair to my mom, Nelly was blasting on the radio. I'd listen to "Hot in Herre" over some complaining little kid, too. Also, it was 2007, so people didn't get just how bad secondhand smoke was for you yet. Doctors were like, "That little tickle in your throat? It's real cute, ain't it? That's called puberty, son. You'll grow out of it."

I sighed and pulled my shirt tighter around my face. "Your window. Can you roll it down, please? This smoke is killing me."

She shrugged. "Oh. Why didn't you say so?"

And she rolled it down like half an inch.

"There," she said, taking a deep drag. "Happy?"

Totally. A real Hallmark moment. My heart was warmed, and my lungs were crispy.

"Yeah," I said, staring out the foggy window. "Thanks, Mom."

When I look back on it now, I'm like—yeah, I get the whole small-town thing.

The town I'm from in Ohio, North Lewisburg, is about an hour west of Columbus, but it is rural as hell. I always tell people that Ohio is the Alabama of the North—we are so trashy you wouldn't believe it. I mean, no offense to the good people of Alabama, I guess. Even without the cigarettes, my mom has that southern twang. She sounds country as fuck. If anything, I'm lucky she picked cigarettes as her drug of choice and not heroin, which at this point was kind of like the city mascot. Just a big cartoon needle with a smiley face posted on the one road into town. "Welcome to North Lewisburg! Where life just dissipates!"

But there are some pros to the small-town experience, too. While I was growing up there, North Lewisburg had about fifteen hundred people. It was literally a one-stoplight town, which could've easily been a four-way stop, and you had to drive through twenty minutes of farmland just to get to that one stoplight.

Everyone knew everyone else. You could honestly leave your keys in your car's ignition overnight, and not just because you're a dumbass who forgets his keys everywhere, but because you knew your car would be safe. Not because small-town people are any more honest than big-city people, but because you couldn't get away with breaking a law if you tried! What are you gonna do? Steal your neighbor's car and park it down the street? Everyone's watching everyone else, everyone's in each other's business. You take something and *we will find out.* So yeah. It was safe. It was a tight-knit community.

And there was a lot of nature outside. That was cool. Trees to climb. Creeks to play in. Cornfields to run through. Lots of sticks—or swords to a kid with the right imagination. The joy of being a child—I'm pretty sure that's somewhere in nature, right?

Yep. Definitely a few pros to small-town living.

Honestly, though, back when I was growing up there it was mind-searingly boring. This is the kind of place where the gas station is also the country store, and maybe they run a pizza joint out of the back. So everyone around me was either a mechanic or they worked in the pizza place, and the cool thing for them is there's like zero commute. Fuck around, you get some sandwiches, some diesel, maybe a pepperoni on the side. You got the car guy working on the pizza guy's car while he's eating the pizza guy's pizza, and they're both buying corn from the farmer, who also happens to really like pizza and broken cars. And that's about it.

The farmers were actually the closest thing our town had to fancy people, because some of them actually made decent money. There was no bigger flex than driving down the single street through that single stoplight on a brand-new decked-out John Deere. Polished green and chrome with a three-point hitch and a rotary tiller—size does matter.

Life pretty much went like this: you go to high school, you get pregnant or get someone pregnant, you graduate high school, you get a job, you get married, you get someone else pregnant (maybe your wife and maybe not), you work some more, there's a few more pregnancies, and then you die. Once you die, you may stop getting pregnant, but seriously? No guarantees.

Everything was the same, everything was normal, and everyone was white. Well, that's not true. There were three Black kids, and they were mixed. Brendyn, Derick, and Devin—they were my best friends, and they were all related. They just happened to live next door to us, which was a dream because in a small town like that, it was really just a matter of "whose door can I knock on next? I need friends!" We didn't have phones, and social media was only just getting started, so if we got tired of playing in the creek or running through the cornfields, we'd race our bikes or sit on the power boxes in the backyard until the lightning bugs came out.

Maybe if I'd had a better homelife, I would've felt a little more rooted to the Alabama of the North. But I didn't.

When I was a year old, my dad killed himself. He was only twenty or twenty-one at the time. He and my mom weren't together then, so he was staying with his own dad in this shitty little apartment, and yeah, he just shot himself. Now, I know your first natural human instinct is to feel a lot of sympathy for me. And that's very kind of you. Your second natural human instinct is to be like, "Yo! You're a comedian! Stop being so damn depressing!" That's a little less kind of you. I'll accept a middle ground.

But seriously—I was just a baby when all this happened. Could barely even walk. I have almost no memories of my biological father. In fact, I'm not even sure how I found out the way he died. I'm thinking that my mom maybe broke the news to me when I was around seven or eight—maybe—but let's be honest here: Is the news of your dad's suicide really something y'all would be dwelling on in *your* life?

I think I'm gonna focus on those memories of catching crawdads in the creek, thanks. And all those sticks outside.

What ended up hitting me a lot harder—I mean literally, this dude hit me—was the *next* guy my mom married. A guy I shall simply refer to as That Asshole. That Asshole happened to be both a mechanic *and* a pizza delivery dude in our town. No bullshit. He was a real dual-threat in the local job market.

I have no idea how exactly my mom met him, but what I do know is that one day I got home from daycare and my mom tells me we're moving to the middle of nowhere, this town called North Lewisburg, with this tall guy with a big nose, a goatee, and a buzz cut. His hobbies were limited to sitting on our couch, pounding Bud Lights, and watching NASCAR. And on no planet was

I allowed to change the channel to any of my own shows or play PlayStation. I was to sit there quietly, respectfully, while he watched those cars go around and around in circles, drank his beers, and tossed one empty can onto the floor after another. And another. And another.

That Asshole.

As I got a little older, I got more angsty and hormonal and confrontational. That's right—teenage boys, we're pretty fucking bad, too! I wouldn't go out of my way to start things with him, not necessarily. It would just be dumb stuff like:

"Matt, I told you to pick up your shit off the floor."

"All right, bro. I'll pick up my shit—just as soon as you pick up all your beer cans."

"What the fuck you just say to me?"

"You fucking heard me," I'd say under my breath, walking away, hoping he didn't hear me but wishing he did.

You know, pure adolescent poetry. He'd go to smack me upside the head, and I'd try to smack him right back. And, well, I'd get my ass whooped. What do you want from me? I was this skinny little punk! I might end up with a few bruises, maybe some of my clothes would get ripped in any wrestling match—*"Dammit! That Hooters: Daytona Beach shirt was vintage, dude!"*—but I was so small that most of the time That Asshole would just pick me right up off the ground and throw me into my room.

We lived in a few different houses over the years: a trailer, a farmhouse that we rented, and a couple little houses in cul-de-sacs.

7

But I always felt like the odd man out. In some ways literally. I had three stepsisters and one younger half sister, and they mostly acted like I was just in the way.

My mom didn't have any great solutions, either. When my stepdad and I fought, sometimes she'd break it up, sometimes she wouldn't. It kind of just depended on how bad it got. But what could she do? He was a grown man, and she was smaller than I was. She was a stay-at-home mom with a strawberry blond perm who'd had me when she was twenty years old, just out of high school. The most work she'd ever done was as a mailman for a couple years— a mailman!—which, come to think of it, was probably the only other job besides pizza guy, mechanic, and farmer in the town of North Lewisburg, Ohio.

She loved and cared for me and my little sister so much. Sometimes almost too much. It could feel like we were her whole life, like all her needs and wants were this thick-ass wool blanket piled on top of us. That can be snuggly and warm, but sometimes— sometimes—it can be a little hard to breathe, you know?

The closest thing I had to a true savior was my mom's dad, my grandpa Steve. Man, I adored that guy. And he did just about everything he could to make my childhood better. But when it comes down to it, no one can really fix life in rural Ohio. That's why even from a young age, I knew I needed to get out. I also knew I didn't have a future in boxing or MMA. I just had to figure out what that future would be, and where it would take me.

Wherever it was, it needed to be far, far away from here.

———

I didn't know it yet, but as I got out of my mom's gray, rusty Jimmy that morning in the seventh grade, I was about to take a big step in the right direction. It was all gonna start on my very first stage—which just happened to be the dusty gym floor of my tiny, redbrick junior high.

I slammed the truck door behind me. I smelled like an air traffic controller going through a bitter divorce. And my mom? She immediately rolled her window all the way back up. I gotta give her credit, though—as doctors started figuring out just how bad secondhand smoke is for people, she totally changed her ways.

These days she'll roll that thing down a good three inches if you ask her nice enough.

2

WALKING RED FLAG

All right. I had it. The idea for the perfect bit.

"Mrs. Haye!" I shouted, waving my hand around in the air. "*Mrs. Haye!*"

It was first thing in the morning, and I was in seventh-grade homeroom. To most kids, this was just where they took attendance and made announcements. Time for a little socializing, a little gossiping, maybe finishing up some homework. Boring shit like that. And to be fair, that last one could also be me, because I always did my homework, because I was a big-ass nerd.

But because I was a big-ass nerd, I also had big-ass aspirations. I wanted to be the class clown. And there was no better place to try out new material than homeroom.

"Yes, Mr. Rife?" my homeroom teacher said, eyeing me suspiciously. What can I say—I was already starting to earn a rep.

"I—I think my contact just popped out," I gasped, all nerves and anxiety as I searched the top of my desk and then the floor. "Oh wait! Wait! Here it is! Found it!"

"Oh, did you," she said dryly.

"Yeah! It's right here in my hand. See? Hey, could I have a hall pass so I could go to the bathroom and put it back in?"

"Matt?"

"Yeah?"

"You realize you're wearing glasses right now, right?"

"Oh! *Am I???* I had no idea!" I looked around the room triumphantly at my fellow classmates. Like, *Did you guys just see that? I tried to get a hall pass for a missing contact—and I'm not even wearing contacts! I'm wearing glasses!!!*

A few kids rolled their eyes. Someone cleared their throat. Maybe I got a few chuckles. Maybe.

"Matt," Mrs. Haye said with a sigh, "please take your seat."

Okay, fine. It doesn't take bifocals to see that routine could use some work.

One of my first breakout bits as a comic—one that went just a tiny bit better than my infamous childhood "I'm not wearing contacts!" number—was about red flags in dating.

If you don't know, it's basically a warning sign. A metaphorical stop sign. You meet somebody, you start talking to them. And there's something about them that just kind of triggers a warning in you. Like, maybe this isn't a person I should be fucking with, right? I have so many of these things when it comes to women—I mean, who doesn't, right? If you're a girl who fucks with boats, I'm gonna assume they come with crabs. Deuces. Or maybe you've got distinctive physical features? I don't care if you're a twenty out of ten, if your second toe is longer than your big toe—you're toe-tally out. You got guy "friends" who want to fuck you, but you refuse to believe they actually want to fuck you? Nope. Naïve. Not having it.

And, of course, some of the best, weirdest red flags I've ever heard came from the ladies themselves. The ones in my audiences, I mean. Please explain to me why flip-flops or liking dogs over cats is a deal-breaker with an Ivy League investment banker. I mean, you hate an animal who's literally man's best friend, and *he's* the problem? Come on, now.

But here's the thing. When I was growing up, I didn't just *have* red flags. I, Matthew Steven Rife, was a walking, breathing, human red flag.

None of the usual cliques wanted me. I actually played sports like football and baseball, but the jocks wanted nothing to do with me. All the hot, popular people had zero interest in my gap-toothed face. Even the nerds didn't accept me—and I was a nerd! You know you've got issues when the losers are like, "Sorry, bro—we just don't want any of what you got to rub off on us, you know?" And it's not like I was the new kid in our junior high or something. My school was tiny, just a couple hundred kids in the whole thing, and these were all kids I had known since kindergarten.

I was just different. I just didn't fit in. We weren't exactly well off, which meant that not only was I wearing Kmart "I'm With Stupid" shirts by myself, but I was mixing them in with the same pair of grass-stained jeans every day. I mentioned being small, I mentioned being younger, I of course mentioned my tiny-ass teeth, which were the bane of my existence, but this wasn't just your typical "Oh, I'm a half-inch shorter than everyone" stuff. This was borderline a medical condition. For some weird reason, puberty seriously did not end up hitting me until I was like twenty-two years old.

It was . . . uncomfortable, to say the least. I kept getting older, but it felt like my body was staying the same age. My voice was a little higher, I didn't have to shave at all—even now, at almost thirty, I would say my mustache is more, like, aspirational. It has hopes. It has dreams. It knows what it wants to be someday. Someday. But today? It is not at all prominent. It's more like a whisper of a dare of actual facial hair. But hey, never say never. (Thanks, Biebs!)

And you know what? I ain't complaining. In my business, most people would kill to keep looking young as they grow older. But back in junior high and high school? When everyone else is growing up and getting pubes? *Awkward.*

In hindsight, though—not a bad thing. Being different is what gave me my personality. I am well aware that I currently look like every fuckboy ever. But I didn't grow up that way, and I still identify as an ugly person. I swear—even though I've got veneers, which make my teeth look more or less normal, to this day I almost never open my mouth when I smile for photos. And thank God for that attitude! Think about all the good-looking people out there who know they're good-looking. No one likes 'em! You think they had it easy in life. You think they don't have problems. And honestly, sometimes they act like it because they know all the normal ugly people would give their left kidney to be them or be with them.

Well, that wasn't me. I wanted to stay just low enough on everyone's radar so I wouldn't be bullied—you never want any of the popular people to think of you as a threat—but I wanted to be funny enough so I was always kinda welcome everywhere. No one is jealous of the class clown. He's the comic relief. He lightens the mood. He gets to weave in and out of every social circle. No one wants to get fingered by the class clown on a field trip, but no one's looking to break his fingers, either. I call that a win.

Plus, all the funniest shit happens to us ugly people—ugly people out there, y'all can back me up on this. And good-looking people, watch your backs, because you're totally outnumbered.

Like, I may not have had a group or clique, per se, but that just meant I valued my few good friends even more. My family life was shit, so *they* became my family. And my best friends' family just happened to be Black. Like I said, that started just as a coincidence—they lived next door, so they were the easiest kids to hang out with.

But it also turned out we had something in common—and yeah, it wasn't our preferred SPF. We did, however, all feel like outsiders in our little town. Them as the only Black people, and me as this eternally prepubescent kid with an abusive alcoholic stepdad. To this day, almost all my friends are Black, and the one who's not Black is Russian, and they're basically the Black people of white people.

My Black friends taught me something at that young age, and that's what is by far the greatest, most sincere love language out there—the roast. We would go back and forth for hours, just fucking with each other. And not all of them were clever, not all of them were even very good. I mean, we were just kids. But every now and then . . .

"Yo, Matt! You're the only person I know who can chew their food without opening their mouth!"

Ouch. Fuck.

Merciless, right? But who you think did me dirty like that? My greatest enemy, or my best friend? That's right—it was my best bud in the world, my brother from another mother, Brendyn. Like, he and I were best friends since kindergarten, that's how close we were. And that's also how he knew my teeth were my biggest insecurity. My Achilles heel. Except, you know, in my mouth.

Now don't get me wrong—we were just kids having fun. We weren't sitting around trying to be profound or some shit like that. But on some level, Brendyn and my friends understood that if you feel like an outsider, the best way to deal with it isn't to hide from it, it's to own it. The truth is that all of us—even the annoying hot people of the world—have weaknesses. We all have parts of our bodies or our personalities we're embarrassed of. Usually it's stuff no one else actually notices, but of course we think it's all *anyone* notices *all the time*. Your best friends are there to call it out, to set you straight, to remind you we're all just human and who the fuck cares? You gotta be *proud* of who you are, including what makes you different.

The most painful stuff can also be the funniest, because it hits so close to home. And your friends, the people you have the deepest connections with—those are the ones who know how to get the biggest laughs out of you.

Was I ugly? You're damn right I was! And I had fun with it. I joked about it. I laughed at everyone else—*and* at myself. That's where true power comes from.

Same goes for me and girls. Or the lack thereof.

I got subzero interest from the girls at my school. Honestly, it was so bad I've blocked out all of my multiple rejections. I had two kisses from fourteen to seventeen years old. And both of those experiences would be big enough red flags to ward off any girl with a pulse.

In ninth grade, after years of disappointment, I finally found a girl who would at least go out with me. No shocker here—she went to a different school. I mean, everyone at my own school already knew me as the harmless, earnest class clown. I wasn't going to be changing anyone's mind anytime soon, even with fire material like "Where's my nonexistent contact lens?" What did I finally do? I went online.

These were still the early days of social media. Twitter seemed like it was made up of five total people, and one of them was Ashton Kutcher (accomplished authors like me call this foreshadowing, people, but we'll get there). Facebook had only just expanded beyond the snobby university crowd to include white-trash punks like me. And MySpace still, like, existed. So the internet felt like a window to another universe. Or, you know, at least something different than playing with a stick. Pun intended.

That's how I met . . . let's call her Numero Uno.

Hey girl! Yeah—I know most schools go for jocks, but the kids at my school actually prefer a sense of humor and a total lack of body hair. In fact, I don't even know what I'm doing online in the first place, that's just how popular I am in real life. Now please, I'm begging you to hang out with me. PLEASE!

Numero Uno—which, in case you haven't figured it out, is actually not her real name—was the friend of a friend on Facebook, and she lived thirty minutes away, which was far enough to pretend I was a lot cooler than I really was. She, for her part, was stunning—at least in her photos. She was part Colombian, and a lot cuter than any of the girls at my school. I kinda had no idea what I'd do when she met me in person and saw me open my mouth to speak. But I figured I had to shoot my shot sooner or later, you know? So I asked her out to a movie, to see *Prince of Persia.* Because if epic tales of Jake Gyllenhaal in a cut-off leather shirt and spray tan couldn't get *her* wet, at least I know *I'd* be bricked up.

Honestly, though, I can't even comment on my dude's acting. Numero Uno ended up being just as pretty in real life as she was in her profile—an internet miracle!—and the whole time I was sitting next to her in the dark theater, all I could think was, *What do I do now? Do I hold her hand? Is that too much? Maybe I should just touch her knee with my knee? Just, like, for a second, before she even knows it. But which knee? Left? Right? And how hard should I touch it? Wait—did she just brush my wrist with her hair? Or was that just a kernel of popcorn falling out of the gap between my teeth? Goddamn these motherfucking teeth!*

Anyway, I *finally* got up the guts to hold her hand. Like two minutes before the credits rolled. Yeah, I didn't exactly last very long. And that was just the beginning of "Matt Rife Shows You What NOT to Do on Date One."

We got back to her place. I was still too young to drive, so my grandpa was on his way to pick me up. Numero Uno and I were standing out front awkwardly, just like . . . standing. Like if you thought my brain was going nuts inside the movie theater, out on her front step it was nothing but "AAAAAAHHHHHHHHHH-HHHHHHHHHHHHHHHHHH!!!!!!"

And then suddenly, right before my ride arrived, it was like we both decided at the same time "Fuck it, let's kiss NOW"—and we completely bombed it. I went in for the kiss, but I was really going for more like a little peck, right? Because why would this cute girl want to straight-up make out with me? But she, for reasons I still do not understand, just came at me all open mouth and tongue. Like, Numero Uno was *committed* to a full-on, high-impact, French-style Colombian kiss.

Meaning that this incredibly attractive, out-of-my-league girl just ended up eating a big ol' bunch of my not-yet-grown-into top lip.

Numero Uno, I have no idea where you are now, but if you ever come to one of my shows and you scream out "Guys who take you to *Prince of Persia* are a red flag!" you will not get any argument from me, girl. Not even for a second.

My first kiss was such a bust that I didn't try anything with any other girls for years after that. Basically not until I lost my virginity with my first girlfriend right before I finished high school—you remember her, the girl with the sophisticated body art. And that experience was only *slightly* better than my first kiss. Slightly. And it lasted just about as long, with an equal number of positions and possibly inferior technique. Though at least we had the comforting shelter of her rusty Honda.

Think about it, all right? Those were my romantic *victories*. That awful first kiss was a *win*. But again—think of how dull, how generic it would've been if I was just some random popular jock who knew exactly what he was doing with girls. *Oh wow— another Saturday night, another hookup. Maybe I'll actually watch Jake Gyllenhaal instead.* It was hilarious exactly because it was so depressing. And by the way, none of those "successes" had even happened when I was in the seventh grade.

In the seventh grade, I was nothing but Matt Rife, the Walking Red Flag—heading into homeroom first thing in the morning and trying desperately to work my way up to official class-clown status with revolutionary bits about missing eyewear. I had no goals. No identity. Definitely no self-confidence.

But all that was just about to change.

Back in class, I sat down in my seat after Mrs. Haye denied me my treasured hall pass. She was clearly jealous of my budding talent.

My friend Amanda turned to me. This was another kid I'd known since kindergarten. All part of the same tiny town, everyone's families knowing everyone else's, all growing up together. So in a sense she knew me about as well as anyone, I guess. Which meant she also probably knew I was kind of an outsider, that I never really belonged to any specific clique.

Maybe that was why she asked me what she asked me then. Or maybe after seeing my lost-contact-lens routine, she was like, "I *really* hope Matt has a decent fallback plan." Whatever the reason, she looked at me and said, "What do you want to be when you grow up?"

And somehow, for some reason, I said, "I think I want to be a comedian."

Now, it all could've ended right there. Because honestly, how often did y'all tell *your* friends you had some random-ass dream when you were a kid? If we all kept our word, the entire nation would be filled with nothing but astronauts, firefighters, football players, and princesses. Well, "comedian" could've easily been my very own "astronaut."

But then Mrs. Haye did me a solid. She made up for shutting me down a few minutes earlier. She looked out over the classroom and said, "We're having a school talent show if any of you would like to sign up!"

Look at that—my first real opportunity. My first tiny shot at achieving a gigantic dream I barely even knew I had just a few minutes earlier. Sure, I was just in junior high. Sure, my "stage" would be nothing but the floor of the school gym, and my audience would be a pack of unruly seventh graders. But you remember what it was like at that age, right? *Nothing* feels bigger, *nothing* feels more important than whatever you're doing at that moment. As far as I was concerned, if I got this talent show right, I'd be well on my way to international stardom. At least in rural central Ohio.

3

LOVE STORY

I walked into my small, redbrick high school on the morning of the talent show, prepared for battle.

Hair: gelled. Pants: enormous. Shoes: Skechers. I was built like a young lesbian and dressed like a member of Limp Bizkit's entourage. That's right—I was basically every earnest white-trash performer who's ever been kicked off *America's Got Talent*. And I mean the ones who don't even make it past the opening cattle call. The guys who aren't even weird or interesting enough to get airtime.

But I was determined to have my moment in the show at the end of the day, even if Principal Huffman looked a hell of a lot more like the *Family Guy* than Simon Cowell. This was the first time our school had ever put on a talent show like this. It felt like it was all meant to be. I was only in the seventh grade, but I already thought that maybe, just maybe, stand-up could be my thing.

I just had to get, you know, good at it.

My homelife with my mom and That Asshole was such garbage that comedy had served as a refuge for me for years. I would literally fall asleep each night in front of the flickering lights of Comedy Central. This was way before streaming, so the station would just show reruns of *Comedy Central Presents* on repeat, over and over again. Which meant that for better or worse, comics like Lewis Black, Marc Maron, Christopher Titus, and Dave Attell were bigger role models for me than my actual parents. Probably better, which now that I think about it, may actually be more depressing.

This was the height of Dave Chappelle and Dane Cook. These guys were absolutely killing it on TV and stages all across the world, and I was obsessed. Comedy, for them, wasn't just a job. It was a way of life. A way to connect with people, to communicate. They didn't have to worry about finding a group or joining a clique—every single person in America wanted to be friends with *them*. They transcended stupid labels like "popular" and "jock" and "nerd," all because they knew how to make people laugh.

The week before the big talent show, I sat in front of the computer at home and started searching online for the best knock-knock jokes I could find. Pro Tip: There ain't any. But I didn't give a crap. To me, this was like my Rocky vs. Drago movie montage. Each stupid fart joke was me punching a giant slab of frozen meat. Each new poop gag was another step through the icy tundra of

Siberia with a tree trunk tied to my back. Every awful sex pun was another push-up on my bloody bare knuckles.

And if those classic movie references just went completely over your head, then I suggest y'all get the fuck off social media and watch some good ol'-fashioned TV like real red-blooded Americans. WOLVERIIIINES!!

So yeah. I should've been ready. But by the time the big show rolled around that afternoon, my confidence was shot and I was nervous as hell.

There I was, standing in a big dusty gym with fluorescent lighting that seemed designed to make my twelve-year-old skin look as pasty and oily as possible. I was "backstage"—on the side, underneath the basketball hoop near the cinder block wall—rocking back and forth on my heels, all jittery, and about to get up in front of a hundred rabid adolescents who'd only ever known me as a skinny punk with bad teeth who desperately didn't want to get bullied. In case you weren't aware, kids are the harshest judges out there, except for maybe kids who know you. They're ten times worse.

And the competition I was about to go up against was a murderer's row of preteen talent. I mean, sure, all the teachers kept saying it absolutely *wasn't* a competition. "You're all winners! Just for trying!" But come on—we all knew that was bullshit. All of junior high is one big competition. Hell, all of life is one big competition. Of course it was a competition! All these acoustic guitar players, angsty emo singers, and pre-TikTok dancing amateurs wanted to slaughter me!

I was the only one brave—or stupid—enough to actually try comedy. Almost everyone else was doing some kind of music or dance number. And let's be honest, guys—anything involving music is so much easier to perform live than comedy. It just is! For some reason, if you get up on a stage and try to make people laugh, they don't just laugh and applaud if you do something *right*. They will absolutely tear you apart if you do something *wrong*. A bad joke isn't just met by silence or polite clapping, it's met by heckling, by insults, by f-bombs hurled through the air. And that's just from the faculty.

But music, on the other hand . . .

"Okay, students!" Principal Family Guy announced. "Everyone pipe down and give a warm welcome to our first act of the afternoon, performing a guitar solo he composed himself . . . Chad!"

Chad. Of course his name was fucking Chad. This Chad dude went on to miss every other chord on his guitar—at least I assumed he did, because I could not tell what the hell he was playing, and I doubt he knew either—but did the audience care? No! They cheered this motherfucker like he was Kurt Cobain back from the grave!

It's cool, Matt, I thought, a phony closemouthed smile plastered to my face. *Of course they like him. It's music. Besides, every comic needs a decent warm-up act. You're fine.*

A few more acts came and went. More music. Nothing awful, but nothing mind-blowing, either. Basically, a whole bunch of Chads being their Chad selves. It was almost my turn to perform, and I'd be able to get up there with the crowd engaged, but not *too* blown away—just the right vibe for me to make a strong impression. And then . . .

"Now," Principal Family Guy announced, "let's hear it for Veronica!"

Yep. Veronica happened.

Pretty much every school has a Veronica, right? You know the girl. She's cute, kind of has that girl-next-door look, and she is the *best singer* in the whole school, and somehow everyone knows it. "Oh wow, did you hear Veronica sing the national anthem before the JV quiz-bowl's fundraising barbecue? She was *ah-mazing*."

"Yeah, and then she did the Canadian national anthem after that, and the Portuguese national anthem after that, and Ohio's state song, and I didn't even know Ohio had a state song, and none of us are Portuguese, but she was *ah-mazing* at all of those, too!"

"She really does sing a lot, doesn't she?"

"Yeah, like all the time. Kind of obnoxious."

"But still, she's always—"

"AH-MAZING."

And this means absolutely nothing in the grand scheme of things. Seriously, I know we're supposed to nurture the hopes and dreams of the youth and all that, but everyone knows that Veronica might be middle-school good, but she's not *that* good. She's probably more Golden Corral than *AGT*'s Golden Buzzer. Which is fine! There's nothing wrong with that. That's life.

That also might be why everyone always worships the school Veronica while she's still in school. Because deep down, we know that *this* is her time, *this* is her moment, and it probably ain't gonna get much better than this. So let's celebrate it, y'all! Let's cheer our brains out when she gets up at the talent show and does a Taylor Swift cover.

Which of course is exactly what our Veronica, the real Veronica, did.

"'Love Story,'" I muttered to myself as her band started to play. Kidding—it was a boombox with a corny instrumental Muzak CD. "Of course her song is fucking 'Love Story.'"

Veronica started warbling those first few sticky-sweet lyrics—"We were both young when I first saw you . . ." Come on, don't even *pretend* you don't know all the words—and guys, I gotta be straight with you. This girl knocked that shit out of the park. Like if Whitney Houston was only addicted to friendship bracelets.

Perfect delivery! Perfect crescendo! Perfect everything! By the time Veronica was belting out shit about picking out white dresses and escaping this town together—bro, there wasn't a dry eye in the house. That included me, and I was the motherfucking comedian! People were screaming, stomping their feet, going batshit crazy. Like, *Fuck*, maybe this chick really *does* have what it takes to make it in the bigs! (She didn't, but that's cool.)

Me? I was standing against the gym's cinder block wall, desperately wishing that somewhere, somehow, I, too, could find my own personal Juliet to love and save and throw pebbles at—and wondering how the *hell* I was gonna follow this act.

But honestly, I didn't have much time to dwell on my fears, because the next thing I knew, Principal Family Guy was calling my name up to the stage.

My palms were sweaty as the principal handed me the mic. I looked out over the sea of adolescent eyes, some of them still red from a performance of "Love Story" so over-the-top that even Taylor Swift would've been like, "Seriously? A little too angsty."

I had to switch the mood, and I had to switch it fast. The first thing I decided to do was not worry about all the stupid knock-knock jokes I had spent all those hours learning. No, what I was gonna do was interact with my crowd. Now, can I remember every single word of what I said? Of course not. I was practically a fucking toddler, so get off my back or I'll scream child abuse. But it went something like:

"Thank you, Principal Huffman," I say, doing my best impression of Peter Griffin from *Family Guy*. "Just so you know, I'm about to say and do a lot of weird things on this stage . . . but I'll be damned if I'm gonna be lectured by a pervert."

That shifts the mood.

Our principal chuckles nervously, like—*Okay, I'll let this slide. For now. And do I really look that much like Peter Griffin?? Dammit!*

I'd just referenced a famous line from *Family Guy*, and it tells the other kids a few things. It tells them I'm one of them, because we all watch the same stuff on TV. It tells them I'm not afraid to poke fun at anyone or anything—including our pear-shaped, mild-mannered principal. And it tells them I'm willing to be inappropriate, even in a school setting, which means they have no idea what to expect next.

Most important of all, it gets me my very first laugh. I ain't gonna claim this was a big laugh. It's not like I walk out there in the aftermath of Veronica crooning about Romeo and Juliet and instantly get everyone rolling in the bleachers. But still. I get a laugh. Or at least a vaguely loud chuckle.

That tells me that the audience is on my side. They trust me. They're along for the ride. It kinda taps into the lessons I've learned from all the roasting I did with my friends. Not just to be fearless, not just to own who you are and all your flaws—but also that the best laughs, the biggest laughs, require trust. Even when Brendyn was absolutely destroying me and my gap-toothed mouth, I knew it came from a good place. I knew he was on my side. That's why I was able to laugh it off. That's part of what made it so funny.

Once I have the audience's trust, I feel even more comfortable integrating them in my act. I pull people out of the crowd to help me with my arsenal of internet gags. I pick one of the prettiest girls in class and ask her if she'll come onstage with me to do the worm— "Excuse me, do you mind doing the worm real quick?"—just because I think it'll be ridiculous. And she says yes! And it *is* ridiculous!

I'm only up there for a few minutes, but the weirdest thing happens. It's like I enter this crazy time slip where clock time both speeds up *and* slows down. It's both so fast, and forever. Everything is flying by, but you're taking in every tiny detail. Every moment is burning right into your brain.

"Okay, you!" I say, pointing to my latest victim—I mean, um, very good buddy of mine. "Come on up here and join me onstage."

My friend walks up, a little nervous, because he has no idea where I'm gonna take this bit. Truth is, neither did I—which is half the fun.

"All right," I say. "Now, you're gonna be my ventriloquist's dummy, okay?"

"Okay?" he says.

"You're gonna sit down right here."

"On . . . your knee."

"Absolutely! And if you happen to feel at all uncomfortable, that's only because I've got my hand up your—"

"THANK YOU, MR. RIFE," Principal Family Guy says, coughing out a laugh and clapping way too hard. "Thank you for that very, uh, *interesting* comedic performance."

" 'Your back!' " I shout. "I was just gonna say 'your back'!"

"Indeed, indeed," he says. "Now let's make way for our next act, ahem . . ."

All right, so I didn't exactly crush my very first stand-up gig. Taylor "Veronica" Swift was the absolute star of the show, and even Chad the Untuned Guitar Guy got more applause than I did. After my set, I didn't walk over to the head cheerleader and dip-kiss her to the slow-clap ovation of my peers. And in fact, no joke, I don't know if my school ever held another talent show ever again.

But you know what? It was all good by me. That one perfor-mance was all I needed. I was hooked on comedy. I was obsessed with stand-up.

The next year, at the end of eighth grade, I was voted the big-gest class clown. And most likely to be on TV. And most likely to run away and join the circus. For the record, I believe I voted for myself for all three. And for best-looking. And for best eyes. And coolest hair. And smartest. And teacher's pet. And most likely to be president. There's also a decent chance I added a special write-in vote for "most embarrassing teeth in the history of the planet."

Wait, wait, hold up. Now that I think about it, I want to back-track real quick and say I only voted for myself to run away and join the circus. Yeah, that one really resonated. And it's honestly a legit fallback option to this day.

(Ryan definitely had the best eyes. Justin was for sure most likely to be on TV, as long as you count *COPS*. And everybody knew Drew had the best hair—even though I'm pretty sure he's lost it all by now.)

As stupid as it sounds, winning those dumb class superlatives meant something to me. I was never gonna be part of a clique, but that was fine—I was my own clique. I was my own thing. I was the funny guy.

That would be my way out of Ohio. That would be my real-life love story. Taylor Swift could keep the white dress and the diamond ring.

4

GRANDPA STEVE

My papaw picked me up from home on a Friday afternoon and the first thing I asked when I got into his truck was what movies he'd gotten us to watch on video that weekend.

"Oh, you gonna love this one," he said with his usual gob of chewing tobacco bulging in his cheek. "It's called *Bad Santa*. I heard it's hilarious."

Santa! I loved stuff about Santa Claus. I mean, what ten-year-old kid doesn't, right? Later that night, curled up on the sofa next to my grandpa Steve in his little one-bedroom apartment, I could not *wait* for the winter wonderland of festive Christmas cheer that was about to pop up on the TV.

A few minutes later, I was watching Lauren Graham screw a grizzled Billy Bob Thornton—um, Santa Claus—while she screamed, "Fuck me, Santa! Fuck me, Santa!" over and over and over again.

Me and Papaw had never seen anything funnier in our lives. We were laughing so hard, tears were pouring down our cheeks, and from then on we'd spend the rest of our lives shooting off our favorite *Bad Santa* lines at each other.

If he tried to talk to me while I was eating something, I'd bark, "I'm on my fuckin' lunch break!" just like Billy Bob. Or if it wasn't quoting *Bad Santa*, it would be the latest Adam Sandler flick—"Hooters. Hooters! HOOTERS!!" from *Big Daddy*—or just plain acting dumb like Jim Varney in our favorite Ernest movies, my grandpa Steve puckering up his lips and twisting up his face and going, "Eeeeeeeeew!"

Now, knowing the way that media and society and just plain humans are these days, I bet a bunch of you out there are going *tsk-tsk-tsk* or whatever noise the PC police make right before they try to get another happy person canceled. Like, *That old man was exposing his young grandson to improper influences! Sex and drugs and profanity and dirty-ass Santas! Call child services!*

"It's called male bonding! Haven't you ever seen *Wild Hogs*?" to quote Rob Corddry in *Hot Tub Time Machine*, another fave. And I'm glad all your self-serving, self-righteous moralizing keeps you nice and warm at night—in fact, I bet you jerk off to it, which is the greatest irony of all—but the truth is that my grumpy, gross, wildly inappropriate grandfather was the greatest parental figure I ever had, and in many ways he probably saved my life.

What matters more? That—or the fact that he helped me have an R-rated sense of humor by the time I was eleven?

Every weekend this guy would drive forty-five minutes to the house where I lived with my mom and my stepdad, That Asshole. I won't even call it my home, because it never exactly felt like it, and he'd pick me up and drive me back to his place near Columbus for the weekend. He did that for me. Every. Single. Week.

Did my papaw know exactly how bad things were with That Asshole? Just how physically and verbally abusive he could be with me? I'm not too sure. I tried not to talk to him about it. I bottled that shit up, the way kids usually do. But I know he never really liked my stepdad from the beginning, and I know he gave my mom—his daughter—an earful about that. My mom loved me, but she also needed her family situation and her marriage to work. I totally understand that. Life is a bitch, especially when you're living in a small town with a couple kids and no job of your own.

I think Grandpa Steve also just had a sense about things, you know? He sensed that I was uncomfortable there. He sensed that I didn't feel wanted. But he wanted me around, every single weekend, and that meant the world to me.

The insanely raunchy movies we watched together were just a nice little bonus.

My grandpa Steve was a simple guy in a lot of respects. He was from Ohio, pretty much the same area I grew up in, raised in this tiny little house that they somehow crammed two adults and four kids into. He came of age in the seventies, basking in the classic-rock era and all its greatest bands—the Eagles, the Beatles, Alabama—which is why it's my own favorite music, too. He grew his dark brown hair down to the middle of his back and kept it that way, only cutting it back about every three years and donating whatever the barber chopped off to Wigs For Kids. He would ponytail it quite a bit, just with a simple rubber band from a grocery store or whatever, and literally the *only thing* this man ever wore was a white T-shirt, Levi's boot-cut jeans, and his brown work boots.

A few years back, I actually took the dude to the mall. I was like, "Papaw, I am about to expand the experience of *your life*. You are gonna fucking wear sneakers." Sneakers! That's all I wanted for this man—just wear some regular goddamn shoes! I bought him a pair, he wore them three times, and then they sat on his bedroom floor gathering dust while he saved them for a "good occasion" that never arrived. I felt like it was a major victory.

I called him "Papaw," but I couldn't tell you why. I mean, everyone has weird-ass names for their grandparents, right? Mawmaw, Meemee, Pewpew, whatever. If anything, I was lucky that I got away with something that sounds halfway normal.

What I did know is that he basically provided me with all the stuff I imagine a dad is supposed to provide his son.

My grandpa Steve would take me fishing at Indian Lake, this little man-made lake about an hour away, where we'd mostly just stand around waiting for something to bite. He played baseball with me and even taught me how to throw a fastball during my brief and totally failed attempt to get in good with the jocks. Grandpa Steve laid tile for a living—didn't work for a bigger outfit, was just a one-man independent contractor who drove an old pickup truck that literally said something like "Steve's Tiles" on the side—and sometimes he'd have to work weekends, so I'd hang out with him on the job. I'd be awestruck at how this skinny fifty- or sixty-year-old dude could carry drywall and sheetrock in and out of houses during our brutal Ohio winters, or use the wet saw to cut tile outside when it was practically freezing. His work ethic was amazing. His skill and craftsmanship were incredible, and he was absolutely my manly, blue-collar hero. He did what he had to do. Period.

And honestly, a lot of the time I was also bored as fuck.

Sitting there, staring at him, yawning, or once I finally got a cheap little flip phone, maybe texting with a few friends. He'd try to teach me a handful of things on the job site, but I couldn't have been less interested. I'd spend whole afternoons, entire days like that, cooped up in his truck or in some stranger's house, just waiting. I'd look forward to lunch when he'd get a break, and we'd have a few short minutes to sit together and share the sandwiches that he'd made that morning, along with some pizza-flavored Combos and a handful of chocolates for dessert.

But let's be straight with each other, all right? As much as I loved the guy—and I loved him more than anything—it's not like our relationship was perfect. Is there even any such thing? If you can look at me with a straight face and say, "I am in love with this person because he or she is absolutely perfect," then I will look right back at you and say, "You are an absolute moron. Or you're lying. Pick your poison."

Here's the deal. The more you get to know someone, the closer you get, the more you understand not only what makes them great, but also their flaws. And my papaw, he definitely had his share of flaws.

A lot of shit had happened in his life that had left him deeply bitter and almost annoyingly negative. Seriously, we'd be driving in his truck, and he'd be going on and on in his gravelly voice about anything he could possibly complain about. Bitching about too much traffic or not enough traffic or why are his favorite stores all in different places now or, you know what, his favorite stores would really be better off if they moved someplace new. I'd be like, "Dude, you are seriously *making up* things to complain about! No one wants to be around someone who just spews negativity constantly! Let it go!" But Grandpa Steve could not let things go. Ever.

He'd joined the navy when he was young, got transferred to Maryland and was moving up in the ranks as a highly skilled airplane mechanic, and then my mom was born right after he turned twenty. He was always big on personal responsibility and honor and all that great shit that no one cares about anymore, so he decided to give up his budding career in the navy for a much-better-paying job as a contractor back in Ohio. He was happy he was able to support his family, don't get me wrong, but I think he always wondered "what if," you know? What if he'd been able to make it out of Ohio and actually made something of himself, what could his life have been then?

And that was just the vanilla ice cream of his disappointment. The cherry on top? The lady he gave it all up for, my grandma, well . . . that didn't exactly end up working out. And when my grandpa and grandma's marriage broke up, it had a real ripple effect, you know? I was maybe nine years old when all this went down, and this was the end of any kind of harmony or unity in my extended family. Celebrating Christmas or Thanksgiving or birthdays together—it all went right out the window. Cue the start of my trust issues.

In one of my red-flag sets, I had a lady tell me that she found out her husband was paying for escorts. Which, yeah—red flag. I concur. That seemed to set off a whole round of women telling me about their cheating boyfriends. Maybe it's because something was in the air. Maybe it's because we were in Miami. There was a woman who said her ex cheated on her while she was in the same bed. Passed out, drunk—so, kind of on her. And another lady who claimed her ex had a threesome with her two best friends, also while she was there. Okay, yeah—so it was probably the Miami thing, if we're being honest. My main response to this level of insane misery is that if you think your life is hard, there's definitely someone out there who's got it way worse. All right, fine. Maybe not much worse than your ex having a threesome with your two best friends while you're in the same room. But still. Worse. Give it some time, and life will get better. It really will.

Well, when my grandpa Steve's marriage came to an end, huge shocker—he did *not* see things that way. Turns out Papaw was not a glass-half-full guy when it came to divorce. He got rid of any of her stuff that she'd left in his place—like, he did not even want to be *reminded* of my grandmother. And he practically became a shut-in. He had a few buddies he knew from construction, sure, but they weren't close. He never went out. He never tried to date. He kept his apartment immaculately clean. Perfectly organized. He was one of those dudes who has covers on all his furniture, which to me has never made sense. I'd be like, "Papaw, why?? The furniture is there for people to sit on it! That is its *purpose*! That's why it was *created*! Why cover it up??"

And I shit you not, he'd look at me and go, "Gotta keep it clean for company."

"COMPANY??!! Dawg, I'm the only other human who comes here!"

His homelife pretty much turned into him sitting around, watching his movies, protecting his furniture, and nursing his grievances. And don't get me wrong—my dude had some legit grievances to nurse. Me, personally—I'm a big fan of keeping a chip on your shoulder. The chip that's on my shoulder currently weighs about a thousand pounds and counting, and if anything, it drives me to work harder and achieve more.

But it's also possible to be overcome by your anger. To stagnate, to let it suffocate you. To get so consumed by hate that you stop growing as a person. I'm talking some real Dark Side of the Force kind of shit. I'm not saying that Grandpa Steve had reached full-on Emperor stage, but he had definitely left his Anakin days long behind him.

In a way, I kind of think he needed me in his life just as much as I needed him.

Around the time I started high school, shit at home got even worse between me and my stepdad. I don't know if he changed all that much, but I was getting extra hormonal. Trying to pick fights even when fights weren't being picked with me. Just a teenager being teenagery.

Who stepped in to save the day? Grandpa Steve, of course.

When I turned fifteen, he said I could try living with him for a year. My mom obviously knew she could trust him, so we decided to see if it would work. He actually moved into a new apartment to make it work, a two-bedroom, and it was basically stuck in the seventies, just like him. Eggshell countertops in the kitchen and all his old furniture covered in the plastic I hated so much. But I'd already been spending my weekends with him for years, so in a sense it wasn't anything new. I even had my own little TV so I could play PlayStation at night. It seemed like the perfect way to get a fresh start away from the rest of my family.

And at first it was. We'd rent our favorite Adam Sandler movies and hang out on the couch, just like we did on our weekends. Grandpa Steve was an amazing chef, so suddenly I was devouring steak and beef stroganoff every single night, instead of the dry-ass pork chops and frozen taquitos I was used to at my stepdad's place. My grandpa also lived in a better school district, so even though I'd left my friends behind, I was supposedly getting this higher-quality education, too.

But after a while it started to wear thin. My stepdad might've been out of the picture, but I was still young and angsty, and my grandpa was a stubborn old man. We started butting heads more and more. Then one night I decided to stay up even later than usual playing *Call of Duty* in my room. Actually, "decided" is too strong a word. I just lost track of time. Yeah, it was a school night, but I just didn't give a shit.

Then the next thing I knew, there was Papaw, standing at my door. "Hey," he told me. "You gotta turn that junk off and get into bed. You got school tomorrow."

I looked him dead in the eye. "Shut up."

His jaw dropped. He was so stunned, I don't think he said a word. To this day I can't believe I spoke to my grandfather like that. It sounds trite, but there was nothing personal or premeditated behind it, you know? I was just a stupid hormonal kid who was tired of being talked to, who had no idea what he was doing that day or what he was doing with his life. So I said something dumb.

It's not like that was the final straw or something. I don't think there was one. The whole arrangement just kind of ran its course. I had lasted maybe a semester and a half there, living with him, when we decided I should probably move back in with my mom and stepdad. It was for the best. For both of us.

I still had a few weeks of school left before the move, and one weekend I was sitting in Grandpa Steve's old pickup truck. Bored. Waiting for him to finish yet another tile job. I started thinking about my dreams of being a stand-up comedian. After that talent show a couple years back, it had all seemed so clear. It had all seemed so straightforward.

"What do you wanna be when you grow up?" my friend Amanda had asked me in homeroom.

"I think I want to be a comedian," I'd answered.

I had done the show. I had gotten up onstage. I had made people laugh. I had decided that I really was gonna be a stand-up. But so what? Where was I supposed to go from there? What was I supposed to do? Keep waiting for more talent shows, losing out to local hometown heroes who could barely play a guitar?

But now that I thought about it, there were other shows I'd heard about, too. Actual comedy shows called "open mics," where pretty much anyone who wanted to, could get up and perform. I'd never been to an open mic before. Hell, I'd never even been to a real comedy show before. I just devoured the stuff on TV. But I was pretty sure I had heard about a club in downtown Columbus, just a few minutes from where my grandpa lived.

I pulled out my phone. Thankfully by then I had upgraded from the flip phone, and I actually had decent internet. I opened up Google, punched in "comedy open mics near me," and there it was. A club called the Funny Bone had an open mic every Tuesday, every single week. I was only fifteen years old—but why the fuck not? What else was I spending my time doing? Staying up late playing stupid video games?

My grandpa opened up the driver's-side door after a long day of laying tile. He sighed, exhausted, and I guarantee you he was getting ready to complain about *something*.

"Papaw," I said, before he had a chance to say a word. "Wanna go to a comedy show?"

He looked at me and grinned. It was on.

5

UNCOMFORTABLY YOUNG

Me and Grandpa Steve rolled up to the Funny Bone in his old "Steve's Tiles" pickup truck.

It was a Tuesday night. The place was small, it was seedy, it was twenty-one-and-up only, and it probably made most of its money selling gallons of cheap booze on any given night. I gazed at the grimy walls and gulped. As far as I was concerned, this was a straight-up cathedral of comedy.

Thank God I was wearing a tie and a backwards hat like a fuck-boy rodeo clown. At least I was dressed like a total pro.

We got out of Papaw's truck and walked towards the ticket booth. Funny Bone comedy clubs are a national chain, and even though the one in Columbus felt a little rundown to me at the time, it's a serious comedy club, and some real names have performed there. Everyone from Dave Chappelle to Drew Carey to Jerry Seinfeld and D.L. Hughley—who I seriously loved back then from his star five-minute-long performance as a bathroom attendant in *Soul Plane*, which I guarantee you I watched on some weekend night with my grandpa Steve.

Yet it had been shockingly easy for me to get a spot in their open mic. And if I wasn't shocked, it was only because I was so naïve I didn't really know any better.

Here I was, a teenager who barely looked twelve. I didn't shave yet, I wasn't old enough to sample the alcohol they sold, I'd never even been to a stand-up show in my life, and what did I have to do to get my name on the list? I just went online, filled out their "contact us" form, which apparently connected me directly to the owner, a guy named Dave Stroupe who I'd never even heard of before, and I was basically like, "Excuse me, sir, I would like to perform at your comedy club. I am only fifteen years old, but I promise I will not try any of your delicious liquor. I will behave nicely and leave as soon as I am finished, and I will attend with a chaperone who is my grandpa Steve. I call him Papaw."

And Dave Stroupe messaged me back something like, "Sure, kid. Whatever."

All I had to do to get a spot onstage was show up at the door—except for one minor hurdle. Like every comic at the open mic, I had to get at least five people to come watch me. Five.

I had Grandpa Steve and . . . Grandpa Steve. I mean, think about it—all my friends were surly children like myself. They couldn't get into a bar. What was I gonna do, call my mom and That Asshole and be like, "Hey guys, I know I tried to move as far away from you as possible, but wanna see if I can make you laugh? I've got this great new bit about my traumatic homelife that you're gonna love!"

It was the biggest night of my life. I had memorized a solid five minutes of jokes—no note cards for me!—and I still had zero clue how I was even gonna get in.

"Papaw, what am I gonna tell these guys? You think if I ask real nice they'll just do me a solid?"

Pro Tip: No one at a comedy club will ever do a teenager in a backwards hat a solid.

"Don't worry," Grandpa Steve said with his trademark chaw in his cheek. "I got it."

Then, while I walked to the back, Papaw went to the ticket booth and bought five tickets himself. These things were twenty dollars a pop. Think about that—a hundred bucks on a tile-layer's pay. After taxes, that's probably what he made in a whole day. And without hesitating, he spent it all on me.

It was a gesture of faith I would never, ever forget. Now I had to prove it wasn't for nothing.

The club was dark with low ceilings, about nine feet tall, which could help amplify any laughter—and any dead silence—plus a small stage with a weird, fake-looking metal backdrop. It looked like you could cram about three hundred people in the place, but tonight there were maybe forty in the crowd, most of them looked like friends of the performers, and they were all getting good and

47

wasted. Which at fifteen was something I couldn't even do to calm the nerves.

The other comics there—the "real" comics, or at least that's how I thought of them at the time—were these older, grizzled dudes. A guy named Rick, the long-time host, looked me over. "You're the kid, huh? Fine. Your funeral. Wait over there at that table."

"All righty, then," I said, shuffling over to sit by myself. "Thanks."

Yeah. Not exactly the friendliest bunch. There was no special movie moment when a gruff but paternal seasoned vet came over and took this young prodigy under his wing, like a stand-up Chubbs Peterson with Happy Gilmore. No one was even missing a damn hand. This was the open mic, so most of the stand-ups were amateurs, some had been performing for a while, and all of them were stuck in Ohio, just like me.

They were bitter, they wanted all the laughs for themselves, and they were probably annoyed that some punk kid thought he could take up their precious stage time. But how many comics can you think of who seem like kind, well-adjusted people? We're all fucked-up. That's why we're comics!

But you know what? It didn't faze me. Even though I was only starting out, I was just as competitive as they were. I was ready for this. I had my tie, I had my hat, I had my jokes. I was a pro-in-the-making, baby! I was cool, I was calm, I was collected. I was—

"Okay, people! Give it up for the uncomfortably young . . . Matt *Reef*!"

—definitely about to shit my pants.

I started walking up to the stage, doing my best to forget Rick's blatant mangling of my last name—*I mean, how hard is it to say "Rife"? It's only one fucking syllable!*—when the gurgling started. And the bloating. And the gross brown liquidy feeling in my gut.

Like, seriously, out of nowhere! I had heard of stage fright before, but I had never experienced it. Hell, I'd never even been on a stage! Was *this* stage fright?! All I could think was, "This is really happening. I am actually about to drop a deuce. In my pants. In front of forty strangers and Papaw."

Then I got up on the stage, and I stood at the mic in front of that stupid fake-metal backdrop, and I was fine. "I know what you're thinkin', I'm not Justin Beiber . . . my hair is cool, and virtually sperm free." Not too bad for an opening line, if I do say so myself. But then, about halfway into my five-minute set of studiously memorized jokes, suddenly my mind went blank. I froze. In fact, the only thing I mumbled was, "I'm freezing up right now." Which, you know—accurate!

Then the strangest thing happened. Someone in the crowd who wasn't Grandpa Steve, one of the strangers I had almost crapped my pants in front of, shouted out, "You got it! Take your time!"

Turned out that even in this fucked-up world, an open-mic audience full of boozy adults will root for a teenage kid stuck permanently in prepuberty. Now that I'm older I actually hate kids. I hate kids so much. It's like we don't click. The only app kids should ever be on is Amber Alert. Period. But it turns out that most normal adults actually like kids. They like it when we hope, when we dream. When we try dumb shit we shouldn't be trying just because we have some silly misplaced faith in the universe. People really dig that kind of shit.

And y'all know what? I have zero problem milking it. I took in that positivity from those forty strangers that night, and not only did I not crap my pants, not only did I finally recover from brain freeze after about twelve seconds and finish my set, I actually had a good time. I got some laughs. And yeah, some of 'em might've been sympathy laughs, but still—I got some laughs. And that's what being a comedian's really about, right?

My grandpa Steve and I headed out directly after my set, just like I'd promised the Funny Bone's owner. We got in the "Steve's Tiles" pickup truck, pulled out of the parking lot, which really wasn't all that full, and started heading back to his apartment.

"Well, Papaw?" I said. "What'd you think? How'd I do?"

The old dude shrugged. "Hell. I thought you was funny."

That's all I needed to hear. He was the toughest laugh I knew.

Each week, Grandpa Steve drove me back to the Funny Bone. Even after I moved out.

In a sense, all the rest of my life just kind of fell away, you know? I kept playing sports, and I actually got a little better, but I stopped caring about getting in good with the jocks. I had my comedy. It was like a hobby, but on crack. Like if I was a nerd building one of those ships in a bottle, it would be some Carnival Cruise shit with a hundred sails, three swimming pools, and at least one shuffleboard deck. I was gonna make it awesome.

I had no idea that comics typically hone the same set with the same jokes for months or even years at a time, so I came up with new jokes every single week. But it was actually pretty cool, because it allowed me to experiment with stuff, find my voice as a performer.

One time early on I decided to try out some physical humor. I can't remember for the life of me what my setup joke was—so yeah, it was clearly killer material—but the main idea was I'd end up having a huge, sobbing, all-out tantrum right there onstage. Fucking brilliant, right? Here I was, a teenage kid who looked about three years younger than I really was, and I'd play right into the stereotype of who I was supposed to be.

And bro, when I got up there in front of those thirty or so people—the open mic was never exactly a packed house—I *sold* that bit. I was *committed.*

I had a full-on, massive breakdown right there and right then. I collapsed onstage, flailing my arms, kicking and screaming and blubbering, crawling along the floor, tearing at my clothes, totally lost in a tornado of wailing and grief and hysteria.

Then I looked up.

Dead silence. They talk about hearing crickets, right? I swear I actually heard a cricket, sitting somewhere way in the back all by himself with his legs crossed, and he was like, "Dude. No. Just . . . no."

Looking back on it, I was probably subconsciously trying to do my version of Dane Cook's notorious "I DID MY BEST!" routine where he cries to no end, which is iconic. But hey, Dane Cook was the biggest comedian on earth, while I was still crying from the growing pains in my knees at night—we were on different levels. As much as I love comedy, I realized that the physical, slapstick stuff was not my bag. I still don't do much of it to this day. You're welcome. I find it terrifying to commit. Cue my second red flag!

But honestly, even with all that work I was putting in, even with all my experimenting up onstage, trying to figure out who I was, I could still be stuck in Ohio trying out new bits in nearly empty clubs if it wasn't for something else I put a lot of time into—Twitter.

Now, it's no secret that even though I owe a lot of my success to social media, I fucking hate. Social. Media. And seriously, can you blame me? (Don't answer that—I know you'll find a way.) No matter what your platform—Facebook or Instagram or TikTok or Twitter or X or whatever you want to call it—it's just become this cesspool of negativity. It's become the worst version of freedom of speech. You can get away with whatever you want, there's no accountability, so it brings out the worst in all of us.

Especially white people. And yeah, I know there's a lot to unpack there, because there's a lot of worst in a lot of white people.

But social media creates a very special space for them to be the worst, because it allows them to both act all woke in the phoniest ways, *and* they get to judge you because you ain't woke enough. It's like the perfect PC one-two punch.

On the one hand, they're falling all over each other online, trying to outdo each other with just how sorry they are about the state of the world and their own whiteness. Like, I voted for Obama! Three times! Oh, and Jesus was absolutely a Black dude. Oh, oh, oh—and my favorite film franchise is *absolutely* Madea.

Got you. Liar. Madea is no one's favorite franchise. Not even Black people's.

Then they'll come after you if you're even the tiniest bit not woke enough for them. Like, I hate to break it to you all, but it's true—I'm a straight white male. It's not my fault. It's not like I made a conscious decision to be born a straight white male. I mean, probably would've. Historically speaking, why not be on the winning team, right? But I didn't get to choose. I didn't do all that horrible shit that white people have done. I'm a new white! Give me a chance! I can't apologize for that.

Just be a decent fucking human being. That's all we can ask. But almost no one is decent on social media anymore, because that's where we go to judge.

But lucky for me, it didn't used to be that way. Back when I was in high school in the early 2000s, Twitter was practically like a little chat room, an actual community. All these famous funny people were just kinda hanging out, like, "Well, I guess this new weird platform is here. Why not?" Even though I was just this young kid slumming it at an open mic in the middle of Ohio, I could shoot my shot to anyone who was listening. Why not? What did I have to lose?

Well, D.L. Hughley happened to be listening.

This was a legit, incredibly successful comic who was literally one of *The Original Kings of Comedy*, along with Steve Harvey, Cedric the Entertainer, and Bernie Mac. He'd also hosted the original *ComicView* on BET, an amazing show with a huge urban following. (Go ahead and apologize because you never heard of it, white people, the sound of white guilt is music to my ears.) I mean, this dude was just a colossal talent.

What's the first thing I ever tweeted at him? "Oh man, I love you in *Soul Plane*." That's right—that movie I'd rented with Grandpa Steve where D.L. played a bathroom attendant for like five seconds.

Though to be fair, it really was an excellent five seconds. So powerful. So fucking poignant. It was a riveting Oscar race that year between him and Chris Rock as the dude who wants a sip of soda in *I'm Gonna Git You Sucka*. Barely beat out by Samuel L. Jackson as the guy who tries to rob McDowell's in *Coming to America*.

For some crazy-ass reason, D.L. Hughley actually decided to respond to this random teenager who called out his brief performance in objectively one of the worst movies of all time. Not only that, but when he came to play the Funny Bone a short while later, he even offered to give me my first guest set. I had just turned sixteen, and thanks to D.L., I got to open his show with a hot five-minute set. Which, by the way, probably *killed* Rick and the other old-timers at the club—which only made it sweeter, of course.

Somehow I managed to hold my own that first night, and I got invited to perform the whole weekend. On the very last night, D.L. honored me, a juvenile delinquent in training, with some of his wisest words of advice. Most of which I promptly forgot, except for his very last line: "And please . . . never mention *Soul Plane* again."

Shit. To this day it's still better than Madea.

As incredible as that weekend was, though, something far more insignificant ended up having the biggest impact on my life. When I first reached out to D.L. on Twitter, we had a fun little back and forth. Nothing huge, nothing crazy, and unfortunately a convo that was lost to the delete button a long time ago—but it was enough to be noticed by someone else. A dude named Gary Abdo, the owner of Atlanta Comedy Theater. That's Atlanta as in Georgia. As in *not* Ohio.

Gary had this weird idea that he could go on social media and somehow find young comic talent that hadn't been discovered yet. I know, right? Fucking insanity. But that's how he found me. I was a junior in high school, only sixteen years old, and just like that I had an invitation to spend the summer down South to appear in a run of shows.

I was about to travel across state lines for comedy. A hormonal, angsty white teenager unleashed without any parental supervision on one of America's biggest—and yeah, Blackest—cities.

6

DODGING BLUE BALLS IN ATLANTA

It was sometime during the night, and I was about to walk into the tiny apartment where I was crashing during my summer in Atlanta, when suddenly I heard a woman crying from behind the front door. I don't mean like little sniffles or gentle tears or some shit—I mean full-on, straight-up, ugly-cry *bawling*.

I thought, *How much weirder can this shit get?*

I was sixteen years old, completely on my own for basically the first time in my life, eating microwave lasagna and cereal every night for dinner. I'd only arrived in this big, crazy, completely foreign city maybe a week earlier.

Gary Abdo, the owner of the club I was working at, had found me this free place to stay. I'd be sleeping on the couch, and the dude I'd be living with was a tall, skinny, thirty-year-old Black comic I'd only met once before in my life for maybe five minutes—but what was I gonna do, turn a free place down? I had no money and no other options.

Then I realized I wasn't just gonna be living with the comic, I was also gonna be living with his girlfriend.

Awww, shit.

She was kinda dark, maybe Middle Eastern in background, and she was cute. Like the kinda cute you think is pretty hot when you're a horny teenage virgin who basically wants to fuck anything that moves, but when you get older you're like—sure, cute. I guess. Also—and here's the clincher—she was older.

I absolutely have such a specific type, and it is older women. If you want, you can read whatever the fuck you want into that. Go on and get Freudian, y'all—I can take it. But as far as I'm concerned, it all comes down to food. A lot of older women have kids, and that just means they got snacks. If you got a Crock-Pot? Girl, I am in love. A woman's perfect age for me is kinda like a bowl of Cap'n Crunch—you want her way after she's gonna tear your mouth up when you take a bite, but definitely before she turns to oatmeal.

Now, I'm not gonna say the comic's girlfriend was the perfect bowl of cereal—she was maybe about thirty, still a little sharp around the edges for my taste—but again, I was young and I was desperate for sex.

And when I walked into the apartment that night, I found her sitting on the couch, the same white couch I slept on every single night—I want to say it was leather, but I feel like my skin would've stuck to it like crazy—and she was just crying her cute-hot-but-not-really eyes out.

I said, "What's wrong? Are you okay?"

And she dabbed at her eyes and said, "I just found out my boyfriend got sent to jail. He violated his parole."

That's right. The same comic I was supposed to be crashing with was now in jail. And it was just me and his very lonely girlfriend together in his crib. I swear to God this happened. No joke. No bullshit. This is not some cosplay role-playing, fuck-your-stepmom bullshit you find on every other Pornhub video. This happened in real life. My life.

Naturally, my only concern is entirely for her well-being, so next I was like, "Do you think I can still crash here? Or do I have to find another couch somewhere? I've got like another two months I'm supposed to be in Atlanta, and, uh, I don't really know anyone else in town, so I could really use the help, and um . . ."

And she looked up at me and blinked and said, "Of course you can stay here, Matt. We'll just have to think of a way for you to earn your keep. A task you can perform for me. A few . . . special . . . chores. But you can stay. Right. Here."

Then she patted the spot on the sofa right next to her—actually, I think it was her lap; yeah, she definitely patted her lap—and I walked over, pulled off my shirt . . .

Okay, so that last part is bullshit. I didn't pull off my shirt. She didn't pat the spot next to her on the couch, or her lap. She was an entirely self-sufficient modern woman, so she definitely didn't need any "tasks" or "chores" performed. And I don't think she actually knew my name. I think she called me Mark, come to think of it. Maybe Max.

But all the rest of the stuff? Him going to jail, her sobbing on the couch and letting me stay. That's all so real.

A few months earlier, when Gary Abdo first pitched my mom on letting her only son go to Atlanta for the summer to hang out in a comedy club, I have a feeling he wasn't like, "Don't worry, miss—he'll get a great education in stand-up and life, and we'll have him sleeping on a couch with a cougar and an ex-con."

Gary's pretty polished for a club owner—always dresses nice, has a dissipating block of dark hair that looks like a Lego piece—so he probably left out the ex-con part.

But even after my mom talked to him on the phone, she wanted to check out the place for herself. I was only a junior in high school. Our homelife may have been kind of bumpy, but she was still my mom, and her antennae may have gone up a tiny bit when I was like, "You can totally trust this guy, Mom! I met him on the internet!" Plus, she was used to having me a short drive away. I had only left the state of Ohio once in my entire life—once!—and that was for a brief stint when my family was living in rural Texas. Yeah, I wasn't exactly a man of the world, and she wanted to see what this whole Atlanta deal was all about.

Plus, Gary wanted to meet me, too. Not only to be polite, but to make sure I was worth the investment. Think of it from his perspective. This dude only knew me from a bunch of funny Tweets and a few DMs we'd exchanged. He'd never seen me perform live before. Gary wanted me to do a set or two in his club so he could make sure I had real potential before he dumped a lot of resources on me.

So during my junior year, me, my mom, and Grandpa Steve piled into her old Jimmy and drove all the way down to Georgia for a weekend. Gary reimbursed us for gas, because he's classy like that. We left at four in the morning, and before we even made it out of the state, we decapitated a possum. Dude ran out to the middle of the road, and we took his head clean off. But hey, no damage to the car, so that seemed to bode well for the trip.

I had never seen anything like the Blue Ridge Mountains as we drove through Tennessee. I'd never experienced anything like America's wide-open plains, the big blue skies that go on forever, the rivers raging and foaming through the land. But most of all, I'd never stayed in any hotel nicer than a Red Roof Inn.

When we finally made it to Atlanta after our nine-hour drive and I saw the Westin that Gary was putting us up in downtown— and y'all, the Westin in Atlanta is fancy as fuck—I was like, "Hell yeah! I am officially never going home." It was a suite! I mean, the bathrooms had fake marble and everything, and I couldn't find one cigarette burn on any of the comforters. Though I have a feeling my mom ended up fixing that little problem during our stay. I gave her the big room with the king-sized bed, and Papaw and I took the two little single beds in the smaller room. Talk about luxury.

Gary's club was the Uptown Comedy Corner, and it was one of the most infamous urban comedy clubs in America. And y'all fucking know what "urban" means, it means Black.

You wouldn't think the club was much by looking at it—this was still the original green-and-black building back in 2011, and it had a very unfinished vibe to it. Like, there was seriously no ceiling, just a lot of random ducts everywhere. But this place was legendary. Some of the greatest comedians of all time had cut their teeth there. Earthquake, Chappelle, Chris Tucker, you name it. And the crowds were both notorious and basically insane.

They'd cram four hundred people in there, and they'd holler, they'd boo, they'd catcall. If they sensed even an ounce of fear, even a moment's hesitation, they'd tear you apart. Comics would trade horror stories about getting absolutely humiliated at the Uptown Comedy Corner. And those were the Black dudes! White comics got *destroyed*. But there was one insult that was considered worse than all the rest.

"The car keys," Gary told me after we met.

"The car keys?" I said. "What?"

"If you really eat shit up there—and I mean really eat shit— everyone starts jingling their car keys at the same time. It gets so damn loud it forces comics right off the stage. So don't get the car keys."

Thanks for the warning, Gary. Super helpful.

There I was on a Saturday night in the middle of Atlanta, this skinny little sixteen-year-old white boy with bad teeth who looked like I was maybe thirteen, and I walked up onto one of the most famous stages in the country, in front of one of the most merciless crowds in the world. The energy was unreal, just thick and loud and bouncing off the walls, off the floor, off the shitty exposed ceiling. I had never experienced anything like it, damn well not at the Columbus Funny Bone. And what did I do?

I ate shit.

I mean, I didn't get the car keys. The audience might've been merciless, but even they weren't going to run a little kid offstage. And trust me—I milked my age for all the pity I could get. But I barely got any laughs. Mostly just a few charity chuckles.

The next day, we drove back to Ohio, my tail between my legs, and Gary called with his decision. "You're too green," he told me. "Develop your material, give it some time, maybe a year or two, then maybe you can try again. You're just too young!"

And maybe he was right. Maybe I was too young. But I also wasn't going to take no for an answer. Because here's the thing—I may have eaten shit up there onstage, but I'd also learned. A lot. At this point I was still writing new jokes every time I performed. I had a core act, yes, but I had no idea how to develop it, how to build on it. I was still experimenting randomly. Gary started to change that. He taught me how to order my jokes to build momentum. He told me about the art of the misdirect, and the rule of comedy always coming in threes. He wanted to be the

Mr. Miyagi to my Daniel-san, I could sense it. He just needed a little nudge.

"Give me one more chance," I said. "There's that comedy festival you have coming up. You already promised I could perform there. Let me do a show. Just one show. That's all I ask."

It was true. He had promised I could do the festival—*before* he saw me perform live.

"Fine," he said, sighing. "You can do the festival."

Over the last few weeks of my junior year of high school, I worked my ass off on my act, applying everything I'd picked up from my short time in Atlanta. Gary flew me back to Atlanta for the festival. It was a budget ticket on Southwest, so I felt like I was already moving my way up. I performed my new set—and I crushed. This was my *8 Mile* moment. No vomiting on sweaters, no Cheddar Bob misfires, just good ol' white-trash redemption.

Gary agreed to bring me back out for the summer. I could feel it. I was one step closer to living the dream.

I was standing in the middle of Lenox Square mall, a place notorious throughout the entire South for selling a lot of expensive designer shit like Louis Vuitton and Fendi—and also for a shit ton of shootings. I was sticking out like a very sore, very white thumb, and I was trying desperately to unload free comedy-club tickets to busy shoppers, using every last drop of my amazing charm.

"Uh, free tickets?"

"Nah."

"Free tickets?"

"Nah."

"Yo, want some free tickets?"

"Nah."

This, I guess, was living the dream.

I'd wake up late in the morning after a late night at the club, eat a bowl of cereal, and Gary would pick me up in his SUV, hand me a huge stack of free tickets to the Uptown Comedy Corner, and drop me and maybe another aspiring comic off at Lenox to hawk our shit, picking us up two or three hours later. Gary was basically a pimp, and I was definitely a ticket whore.

"Come on, free tickets."

"Nah."

"Please, take—"

"Nah."

"Just—"

"Nah."

Fuck! I didn't give a crap if anyone *used* them. I just wanted to get rid of them! They could take a handful of tickets, wait for me to turn around, and just throw the fuckers away for all I cared. Actually, fuck it—I would happily stand there and *watch them* throw the tickets away with a big-ass smile on my face, as long as someone just. Fucking. Took them!

"FREE TICKETS!"

"Nah."

What I couldn't figure out back then was why anyone would turn down something that was free. Like, it's free! Free comedy! Free anything! There is free stuff in the world, stuff that you can get for no money, and a young gentleman with bad teeth is trying to hand it to you, yet you continue to turn it down. Why?? It costs you nothing!

Of course, once I got a little older, I realized that that kind of free stuff—little neon scraps of paper—is some of the most annoying stuff in the world, no matter what it costs. Like, when you walk down the Vegas strip, and some random dude will try to actively force free tickets to strip clubs into your hands. I mean he will legitimately press them into your palm and try to *force you* to grab these tickets. And these are free titties! The greatest things in the world! Free, naked-ass love lumps are being bestowed upon me, as unworthy as I am, for absolutely no reason other than to provide me and my dick happiness.

And what do I do? I push these free tickets—these free, innocent titties—back into his hands or let them drop to the ground and I never, ever think of them again. You know how annoying you've gotta be to spoil free titties?

"Fuck it," I muttered. "I give up."

If the first half of my days that summer were frustrating as hell, the second half were pure bliss. Each night at the club I would soak up as much of the comedy as I could. These stand-ups were nothing like the bitter, competitive bunch I'd met at the Funny Bone. The dudes at the Uptown Comedy Corner were older, they were

Black, and they'd been in the business for years. They were successful in their own right, and they definitely weren't threatened by a little kid like me, so they actually welcomed me to the scene, kinda took me under their wing.

As for the crowd itself, I developed a lot of tools to win them over really quick. I milked the whole "little kid" thing for laughs and sympathy without an ounce of shame—I just didn't want to get the fucking car keys. So I'd be this teenage white boy in the middle of this all-Black crowd, and I'd start making references to anything in Black culture and they would just *lose their minds.*

Mykko Montana booms, and my skinny prepubescent ass comes out raising the roof and dancing.

AHHHHH!

I squeak out some random line from *Boyz n the Hood* in my cracking adolescent voice that is anything *but* hard: "Any fool with a dick can make a baby, but only a *real man* can raise his children!"

AHHHHHHHHHHHHHH!

Or maybe I change things up and go for pure self-deprecation, playing exactly to their stereotype, doing some awkward ultra-white jig to Justin Bieber and "Baby."

AHHHHHHHHHHHHHHHHHHHH!

Other white comics might've been intimidated, but I seriously thought of it as an adventure. It probably also helped that I'd grown up getting roasted by so many of my buddies back in Ohio. Trust me—a crowd of strangers could've never torn me apart the way my best friends did. I was used to being humbled.

Did I kill every night? Hell no! I was still just a kid, but I held my own, I never once got the car keys, and I was learning so much, especially from Gary, who wasn't just the club's owner but had also taken me on as my manager.

When I say he became the Mr. Miyagi to my Daniel-san, I really mean it. He wasn't bald, he wasn't Asian, and he'd probably get his ass kicked if he ever tried karate—but this motherfucker was having me do the weirdest shit. Paint the fence, crane kick, wax on/jerk off. I'm lucky he didn't make me build him a whole new club.

He brought me into the club one afternoon—just me, no one else—he turned off all the lights except the spotlight, turned on the mic, and pointed at the stage.

"Go on," he said. "Do your act."

For anyone who doesn't know, there is nothing more terrifying to a comic than performing in front of an empty house. Give me three people to perform to, even one, and I'll make it work. But in front of *no one*? The whole reason I started doing this was because I live to make people laugh. Live for it! Well, no one can laugh if there's no one in the club. I know—some real Zen tree-falling-in-the-forest shit, right?

"Gary, dude—what is the point of this?" I protested.

"You gotta learn to embrace the silence, man—because there will be times when an audience is silent. And that's not a bad thing."

"I don't know. Sounds pretty fucking bad to me."

"Only if you're not controlling it," he said. "You gotta learn to control a room. Own it, use your timing, use your pacing."

"But—"

"Get the fuck up there!"

And I went the fuck up there, and that's when a tennis ball whizzed by my face.

"GARY! WHAT THE FUCK, DUDE!"

"No!" he shouted. "Don't let the balls distract you! You're gonna get a lot of distractions up there, but you gotta react on the fly! Keep moving, never stand still, keep the crowd engaged, never get thrown from your set!"

"But you almost hit my—"

ZING! Another tennis ball right by a very, shall we say, sensitive area.

"GARY! FUCK!"

"Dodge 'em, goddamnit! Do your set!"

ZING!

"SHIT!"

"You ain't getting off that stage till you do your set!"

ZING!

So that's what I did. I did my set, he tried to peg me with balls—and you know what? I really did learn a lot of control and confidence that day, skills I still use to this day. The only thing I *didn't* do was catch a ball and rip it right back at Gary Miyagi's smug-ass face.

Towards the end of my long summer in Atlanta, I got back to my place one night—I was thinking of it as "my place" by this point—and there he was. The tall, skinny Black comic who *actually* paid for the apartment. And who *actually* had the girlfriend I'd been living with for the last two months.

Fresh out of jail for breaking parole.

I smiled weakly. I only had two weeks left before I had to go back to Ohio. And let's be clear: I never wanted to go back to Ohio. I'd started developing a plan with Gary. Finish up high school early, get the hell out, and move to LA to jump-start my career. But if I wanted to make my plan work, I was gonna have to stay alive first.

What exactly do you say to a dude who just got out of jail when you've been living with his girl? Like, what kind of small talk are you supposed to make? I went with the first thing that popped into my head.

"So! How was jail?"

Subtlety has never been one of my strengths. Like, how was he supposed to answer? "Great, my man—you should give it a try some time, the food actually ain't so bad. So . . . you been fucking around with my lady, or what?"

The honest truth is that the dude never had to worry. First off, I'd never do that to a guy. I'd especially never do that to a guy who's literally in jail. Second, even if I wanted to do something with her, she had approximately zero interest in some random high school kid crashing on her couch, who spent the day passing out free comedy tickets at the mall.

But it was weird. I could sense he was still on edge, so I made things perfectly clear.

"Thanks so much for letting me chill here this summer," I said. "I got really used to sleeping on that couch. By myself. Your girl would just come home every night, grab dinner, and spend the rest of the night in the bedroom. Alone. I had complete and total privacy.

"Did I mention I'm a teenage virgin?"

All right. Yet again, that last line may not be right on the money. But my boy seemed legitimately relieved.

He went on to show his gratitude by spending *five hours* having sex with his girl in the bedroom that night. Over and over and over again. They were very. Very. Loud. And the walls were very. Very. Thin. Not that I can blame him. I mean, this dude literally hadn't fucked in months. And, well, neither had she. They had a lot of pent-up energy.

I guess I'm just glad he took that sexual frustration out on her and not me. Jail can change a man—and I probably couldn't have stopped him.

7

THE LAND OF DREAMS
AND BUS PISS

When I first got there in 2013, Los Angeles absolutely blew my mind.

I mean, picture it. Except for two months living with the girl-friend of a convict and passing out free comedy tickets at a mall where dudes got shot on the regular, I'd spent my whole life in a small white-trash town in central Ohio, where the highlight was pretty much hanging out in my grandpa Steve's pickup truck while he finished laying tile. Before LA, I wasn't even sure the ocean was a real thing.

Now here I was in the entertainment capital of the world. The sun was always out, the sky was always blue, and the streets were all lined with palm trees. The electricity was tangible. People flocked there from every state in the country, trying to break into the business, land a TV show or a movie, and make it big. Me being from Ohio was nothing, just another story in a thousand. Every waitress was fresh off the bus from Iowa and swore she was one audition away from a role in a Tarantino film. Every gas station attendant had just hitchhiked from West Virginia with nothing but a backpack and the script he just knew he'd sell for a million bucks. Everyone in LA had a fucking dream, and it was awesome.

I had no idea back then—no one did, really—but all that was about to change in just a few years. These days, thanks to the glorious miracle that is social media, LA is dead. No one has to go there to act or perform or try to be famous anymore. You can do all that on your phone, no matter where you are in the world! And honestly, you don't even need to have a skill to be internet famous. Don't get me wrong—I'm very aware that social media has been critical to me building an audience as a comic. But at least I *do something*, you know? I have a skill, I get onstage, I tour, I try to make people laugh. Every now and then I succeed. That's how I make my living.

But influencers? People who get paid by products and brands to just, like, exist? They only need to have takes. On anything. The hotter, the angrier, the more hate-filled the better. Any idiot with a TikTok account can scream about something for five minutes and pick up two million followers.

Not back then. Back then, celebrities were celebrities, bro. They were the real deal.

I still remember seeing my first legit celeb out in the wild. I had just ducked into a gas station to use an ATM machine to drain my almost-empty account of its last few dollars—and standing right there was Jonah Hill. *Jonah Hill!*

This was when he was still the funny, cuddly Jonah Hill we all grew up with, back before he got all serious and self-important. And I was just some seventeen-year-old dork from the Midwest, so naturally I went up and asked him very politely if we could take a selfie. And Jonah Hill got this really sincerely tragic look on his face and went, "Oh, I'm sorry, man! I totally would but I'm really running late right now."

And then he went outside and proceeded to sit in his fancy car doing absolutely nothing for like the next ten minutes.

But even then—even then!—I just soaked in the magic of this incredible place. Like, "Wow, I just got blown off by *Jonah Hill*." Then I grabbed a bus to the beach with a bunch of homeless dudes who literally took out their dicks and pissed all over their seats.

LA, baby. LA.

Before I even moved to Los Angeles, I got a warning from a comedian who knew LA better than almost anyone: Don't get cocky.

Growing up in Ohio, I'd always been a huge fan of Erik Griffin from *Workaholics*. He was this big guy with thick-framed glasses and a prominent mustache who kind of came off like a giant Muppet. In his stand-up, he had this way of making everything he said seem kind of charming and personable, but then he'd balance it out with some real shit. Like cozying up to a teddy bear that out of nowhere goes right for your jugular.

And because I definitely *was* too cocky, I pulled the same trick that I'd tried with D.L. Hughley and so many other comics who were completely out of my league—I hit Erik up on social media. In this case, I just up and friended him on Facebook. I didn't bother with any fan-page nonsense, I didn't even send out an opening message. Nope, this was the early 2010s, so I literally just found the guy's personal page and friended him.

Then—again, because it was the early 2010s—we had a poke war.

Fuck. I'm not even thirty yet, but that just made me feel old as shit. It's true though. Me and this famous, successful, talented comedian spent a couple weeks in a poke war. You remember the drill. It was peak passive-aggressiveness.

I'd poke him.

Then he'd poke me back.

Then I'd poke him again.

Poke.

Poke.

Poke.

Nothing but poetry, dawg.

We eventually moved onto actual, you know, words, and I pestered him into agreeing to let me open for him sometime if he ever played Columbus. That didn't come together, but honestly—who cared about Ohio?

Erik lived in Los Angeles. At the heart of it all. Gary Abdo from Atlanta's Uptown Comedy Corner was still my manager, but his specialty was the Black comedy scene. If I wanted to move to LA and break into comedy there, I'd need the help of someone who was plugged in locally. Before I'd even finished high school, Erik offered to spend a weekend showing me and Gary around his town. It was a crazy opportunity to make a good impression.

And at first everything seemed like it was going great. The first day that Gary and I were out there, Erik took us to the club he called home, the Laugh Factory in West Hollywood. This place is insanely famous, we're talking about shows by every star comic from Richard Pryor to Adam Sandler to Dave Chappelle. But it had this really bright, warm, welcoming vibe, which for an outsider like me meant a lot.

Dane Cook just happened to be hanging out when we showed up. *The* Dane Motherfucking Cook. Forget about celebrity—this dude seriously embodied comedy for me. Watching him growing up was literally what made me choose to be a stand-up. This man had changed the course of my life without even knowing it.

And Erik just walked up to him like, "Hey, this is Matt Rife. He's thinking of moving out here to do comedy."

And Dane Cook shakes my hand and goes, "Can't wait to perform with you."

Like it was nothing. Yeah. Pretty much the anti–Jonah Hill.

But when me and Erik and Gary went out to lunch, Erik quickly put an end to my dreams of performing with Dane Cook anytime soon. I was popping off, just feeling myself and everything I thought I was gonna accomplish. I mean, to be fair, I was barely out of high school, and here I was already planning to move to LA, the center of the comedy fucking universe, to blast my career into space. I had reason to be excited!

But Erik just shook his head, looked me dead in the eye, and said, "Dude, you're not funny. You're not a good comedian. You still have so much work to do."

Did I listen to him? Hell no!

I mean, was Erik right? Of course. There was no doubt. But what was I gonna do? Stay in North Lewisburg with my mom and my stepdad? Ever since I'd spent the summer in Atlanta, being in Ohio felt like I was living at half-speed. I was also at a new high school, so I didn't really have any friends. Grandpa Steve, the person I loved most in the world, was encouraging me to leave and follow my dreams. For as shitty as my homelife with my stepdad was, my mom actually didn't want me to leave. She'd been focusing all her energy and all her anxiety on me and my half sister, but if anything, that was just pushing me away. It wasn't her fault, not really—I just felt a little suffocated.

The only real reason I had for staying in the Midwest was sex. I mean, love. Definitely love.

After all my failed attempts at dating, I finally had my first girlfriend. "Never Say Never," who I talked about in my intro. Remember her? Of course you do.

After I lost my virginity to her—again and again and again—I really thought I was in love. What can I say, I'm a hopeless romantic. Every cynic out there is just a romantic who's been smacked upside the head by reality a few times. And trust me—at this point, I've been bludgeoned in the brain more than my fair share.

Our plan was for me to move out to LA by myself, and for her to eventually join me there, maybe enroll in community college. Because we were really shooting for the stars. She, of course, never made the move. We were just young and stupid. But I did make the move. Probably because I was young and stupid. Well, not completely stupid.

Before I made the permanent move to LA, I popped over to take this exam offered in California that allows you to basically test out of high school early. It's not a GED, because you can take it while you're still in high school. As impossible as it might seem, I am actually not a moron. When it comes to academics, anyway. Other things—the jury's still out. But back in grade school, they actually tried to get me to skip the third grade, I was so ahead. My mom wisely was like, "My kid might be smart, but trust me . . . he's also kinda dumb. And already a year younger than his whole class." I stuck with my grade. But I finally got my revenge when I passed the California exam and finished my senior year five months in advance.

Three months later, in January 2013, I moved to Los Angeles for good with $1200 to my name, and I not only convinced Erik

Griffin to believe in me, he even let me crash on his couch for free for a few months while I got my bearings and continued to have totally unrealistic expectations. After that, I moved off Erik's couch and into a tiny apartment with Gary Abdo's son, Cameron. Where I also slept on the couch. Heads up to all aspiring comics out there: Get very, very used to sleeping on couches.

Cameron had just moved out to LA himself after graduating from film school. He was a hardcore cinema nerd, he loved to geek out about classic movies, and he wanted to be a director. Most importantly, he needed a roommate. Except my "room" was a couple shelves we bought from IKEA and pushed together to create "walls" around "my" couch. And yeah, I know those air quotes are doing a lot of work there.

Not that I ever let my living arrangements discourage me from pursuing other, um, opportunities. I finally managed to score a hookup that *didn't* start with an Instagram DM. I caught her eye— I'm sure it was a sexy, but older and wiser eye—from across the lobby at the Laugh Factory and figured I might as well shoot my shot.

"So," she said with a sexy little smile. "Do you have your own place?"

"Uhhh," I said, frantically trying to remember if my roommate Cameron was in town that night. "Yes?"

"Do you or don't you?" she asked.

I cleared my throat. "Yeah, I *totally* do . . . I think."

When we got back to "my place," I tried to take her straight back to Cameron's bed, but she spotted all my clothes piled up by the couch and surrounded by IKEA bookcases. "Oh," I said. "That stuff belongs to a friend of mine. I'm letting him crash for a while until he finds a place of his own. I'm such a generous guy, right?"

I'm not sure if I ever told Cameron that I fucked someone on his bed. But if I didn't—huge thanks, Cameron. The sex was great, and I swear I definitely washed the sheets afterwards.

Dane Cook had no idea what he was getting himself into when— probably as a total afterthought—he casually said the comedic equivalent of "See you around." From there on out, whenever I bumped into him at the Laugh Factory, our conversations went pretty much like this:

"Please let me hang out with you."

"No."

"Please let me hang out with you."

"No."

"Please let me hang out with you."

"You're never gonna give up, are you?"

"No."

Yeah, I got my share of issues, for sure, but perseverance has never been one of them. Dane finally figured he'd kill two birds with one very jacked stone. He loved working out, and it also happened to be the one time he really got to be by himself, so he offered to let me come with him to the gym sometimes. It was a super thoughtful sacrifice on his part, and probably the only way he'd finally get me to shut up. For me it was a huge deal, first and foremost because—I mean, I got to hang out with Dane Cook, this god of stand-up comedy. But also because I had never really worked out in my life.

In my late teens, I was still stuck in my perpetually awkward prepubescent phase. Still not shaving. Still looking like a vaguely stylish lesbian. Still skinnier than a stripper pole—minus the stripper. Maybe if I started lifting some weights with Dane Cook, I could finally put on some real muscle and look more like what I theoretically was—a heterosexual male?

I might've had the right idea with the working-out part, but I was completely off with the choice of gym. Dane's go-to club was Crunch Fitness on Sunset Boulevard, which just happened to be the gayest place I'd ever been in my life. Just, so gay. Crunch was just down the block from the Laugh Factory, which made it very convenient, but it was also in the middle of West Hollywood, which is ninety percent gay. And if you don't believe that statistic, just google their crosswalks.

I would walk into Crunch in sweats and a shirt and immediately be surrounded by these buff-ass men in tights. Like, literally wearing spandex fucking shorts. And they were seedy as hell. That was the other thing about Crunch—it wasn't very expensive. So these guys were basically everyone who couldn't afford to go to an Equinox. It was basically 65 percent gay dudes, 30 percent straight dudes, and 5 percent ridiculously hot women. And every single one of them was trying way too hard.

Dane, though, really had his routine down. It felt like he totally knew what he was doing—lots of machine work, lots of core and ab exercises, different varieties of pull-ups. And I didn't know what the hell I was doing, so I just followed along with him. The only things I did know was that I hated to do legs—it's exhausting, you sweat more, you don't see fast results, seriously what kind of psycho likes to do legs?—and I was never, ever, gonna step a foot into that locker room.

But, you know, slowly I started putting on a little more muscle. And slowly, with Erik's help, I started making a few cracks in the invisible walls of the LA comedy scene. Walls that felt a hell of a lot more real to me than anything in my apartment.

There were a bunch of very cool, very respected stages in Los Angeles. The Improv on Melrose felt very plugged into the industry and was the home of Sarah Silverman and David Spade. The Comedy Store on Sunset was legendary, run by Pauly Shore's mom, Mitzi, and was kind of experiencing a renaissance when I moved out there. And of course there was the indie comedy scene, where you could find literally dozens of shitty open mics at every bar and restaurant with a mic and a floor lamp for "stage lighting." I haunted them all, soaking it in, looking for any opportunity I could get.

But I always gravitated towards the Laugh Factory. From the first time I went there, it had always felt so bright and inviting. It wasn't trying too hard, wasn't snobby or pretentious. The club was just comfortable with who and what it was. And of course, it was insanely important that Erik had an in there.

I quickly figured out that a lot of succeeding in stand-up is just showing up and putting in the time. I'd say it's a marathon and not a sprint, but honestly, you're mostly just sitting on your ass. When I first got to LA, I was still only seventeen, so I still couldn't hang out inside the club. Every night I just hung out in the lobby, chatting up comics like Maz Jobrani and Alonzo Bodden, making banter, getting to know everyone from the door guy to the stage manager, and waiting for my chance.

Until one day a scheduled comic didn't show, and they needed someone to take his place. Erik begged the manager to give me a shot. She was this tall Persian chick named Christina Shams, and she was extremely genuine, which in Hollywood basically made her one of one. Erik's convo with her pretty much went like this:

"Please let him go up."

"No."

"Please let him go up."

"No."

"Please let him go up."

"You're never gonna give up, are you?"

"No."

Christina gave me my shot, and I took my first step to becoming the youngest guy to ever be a regular performer at the Laugh Factory.

But for all the things that were going right, there was also plenty going wrong. Or really just not going anywhere at all. At night, I was usually hanging out at the comedy club, sometimes, if I got lucky, getting five minutes of stage time here and there. But during the days I had pretty much nothing going on. I didn't even have a car—which is crazy in a city like LA, which is this sprawling mess of streets and buildings where no one *ever* walks anywhere—so I spent most of my time hopping the bus and exploring. Heading to the beach in Santa Monica or Venice. Checking out the eerie abandoned zoo in the hills of Griffith Park.

Which might sound pretty cool—and don't get me wrong, I did love all the freedom—but let me be clear: the Los Angeles buses are absolutely disgusting. Just straight-up ratchet. Anyone who's on the bus in LA is just too broke to have a car, or even a fucking scooter. And anyone who's riding the bus during the day? That was just fuckers like me who didn't have a job. I'd see homeless dudes using their seats as their own private (but very public) toilets. I'd spend a half hour or more at graffiti-covered bus stops waiting for my ride to finally show—if it showed up at all. None of those things ever ran on time.

And once I got on? They moved so slow that getting across town could seriously take all afternoon. Usually that didn't mean shit, because it's not like I had anywhere to be. But if I somehow managed to score an audition for some small part in Burbank at two p.m., I'd have to leave at ten in the morning—just to get there in time to find out I didn't get the part.

I was able to make a little money here and there, performing at gigs out of town that Gary managed to book for me, or maybe opening for Erik, but even jobs at respectable clubs only usually pulled in a few bucks. Sometimes the only pay was free drinks—and I couldn't even drink!

Like any comic, my dream was pretty much being able to support myself by performing and not have to take a job in the square world. But after a year and half in LA, shit was honestly looking pretty bleak, even for my low bar. My tiny spot in Cameron's tiny apartment cost me four hundred dollars a month—rent in the city was crazy, even then. By eating nothing but Hot Pockets and ramen, I could keep my expenses down to around two hundred dollars. I was able to get by—barely.

But my LA dream was starting to wear me down. I'd already seen enough in my short time in the city to know that good, talented people burned out of the business all the time. I didn't want that to happen to me. Shit, I wasn't even twenty yet!

Thankfully, though, I finally got a big audition that I knew would change *everything*.

8

REQUIEM OF A
HOLLYWOOD BAG BOY

I was finally there. Gary Abdo, my trusted manager, by my side. The hot, bright lights of Hollywood shining down on me. And the spread they had laid out for me! So much great food to choose from—only the best, really. I had made it.

This was gonna be my big break.

"You need a job?" said the rather rotund manager of Ralphs as she bagged my groceries. "I'll give you a job."

That's right. I was at *the* Ralphs supermarket on Sunset. This place was actually notorious. People liked to call it "Rockin' Ralphs" because it was in the heart of Hollywood, it was open 24-7, and desperate starving artists like me—actors, comics, and yeah, rockers—would come here at all times of the day and night to buy booze or scrounge together a few very-canned, very-processed supplies.

Gary was in town, and he was buying me some groceries, because it wasn't like I could afford them myself. As usual, I was busy bitching because I couldn't find work, because, as usual, nobody would give me a job. Until this blessed angel in our check-out aisle overheard us and offered me the lifeline I needed.

"A job? For real?" I said.

"Yeah," she said with a shrug. "Why not? You'd be bagging groceries, but it would be a job."

I thought about it. There was no part of me that was too stuck-up for any kind of labor, manual or otherwise. I had seen my grandpa Steve work a skilled but blue-collar job his whole life, and he was a proud, good man. At the same time, I hadn't moved all the way to Los Angeles so I could grow old working under the sterile fluorescent lights of a massive, big-chain grocery store. I had come here for comedy, to appear on the biggest stages of the world, to break into TV shows and movies like all my comedian heroes. To live my dream.

That said . . . I desperately needed a regular paycheck. Maybe I could work here during the day and keep performing at clubs at night? Scheduling auditions might be tricky, but it wasn't like I was getting many of those anyway. And who knows? Maybe they'd even give me some free food along the way, or a discount on groceries.

I love to eat, but I *hate* to cook. It makes no sense to me! Why should I plan forty-five minutes in advance for being hungry when I can just go to a restaurant when the mood hits? McDonald's, Sub-way, I wasn't picky at all. Going to a fancy steakhouse was wasted on me—I liked my food simple and quick. Same thing goes for eating at home. If I had to "cook" for myself? It was nothing but sandwiches, ramen, cereal, soup from a can, whatever. If I wanted to get really crazy, I'd do pasta with some kind of sauce I could pour out of a jar. In fact, to this day, even now that I'm no longer living on a couch, I'm a sucker for some frozen foods.

Whenever I get married, I am fully ready to tell my wife, "I love you and I will buy anything for you, but I will *not* cook for you. Ever." Which actually sets me up for success later on. That one time I thoughtfully microwave us a Stouffer's Beef Stroganoff for dinner—I'll look like Gordon Ramsey.

So yeah. Standing in the checkout line at Ralphs with Gary about to pay for twenty packets of Top Ramen, it took me approximately 0.2 seconds to make up my mind and answer the ridiculously nice manager.

"When do I start?"

"See you for training in three weeks."

Nice. Totally nailed that audition.

It was 2015, I was only nineteen, and almost two years into my LA dream. By this point, I'd had a few non-Ralphs auditions. The only problem was that none of them had been even close to as successful as my glamorous foray into groceries.

Auditions for a working comedian can go a couple different ways. Let's say you've got a shot at a stand-up TV show, something that features an ensemble of comics basically doing a few minutes of their act. That's actually pretty simple. You send the producers a tape of your stuff, maybe they bring you in to actually perform your set for them or maybe even for a small, handpicked audience. Each comedian has their own different act, their own bits, and a reasonable chance to get picked to be one of ten people on the show. It's comedy. You just gotta be funny.

An acting audition is much weirder. You go into this random windowless room and compete against twenty versions of you who are all your "type" except better-looking and have been doing this for way longer. You read the exact same part in front of a camera and a casting director who doesn't know you and doesn't really give a shit, but you have to pretend like this is the most exciting opportunity of your life. And then they give the part to one of their friends or some dude they're fucking on the side.

And a *commercial* acting audition? That is fucking weird beyond weird. It's the acting audition but on crack and about car insurance. And the job still goes to some dude the casting director is fucking on the side.

My first big audition was a wild—literally—combo of all three. And it actually took place before I'd even moved to LA.

Right after I finished my summer in Atlanta in 2012, the MTV show *Wild 'N Out* came to Gary's club to hold a casting call. For all you old-timers out there—I say that lovingly, especially to every hot cougar reading this book—*Wild 'N Out* is kind of like my generation's *SNL*, except about a hundred times cooler. It's been going strong for twenty seasons, it's hosted by Nick Cannon, and it's been a launching ground for everyone from Kevin Hart to Katt Williams and Pete Davidson. It also has a ridiculously fun and competitive format.

In each show, two teams of comedians go at each other in what's basically a comedic SmackDown: comics going head-to-head, tearing each other to shreds in a whole assortment of improv games, from the hilariously vicious rap battles in "Wildstyle" to "Twerk Work," where . . . well, I'll just let you figure that one out for yourself. It's a smashmouth pressure-cooker where talent can break through—or breakdown.

And the audition wouldn't be any different. I wouldn't just be doing stand-up or even doing lines from a script. It would be this funky combination of both—coming up with my own brand-new lines for a bunch of the show's games, on the spot, and performing them onstage in front of a panel that included the godfather of it all, Nick Cannon himself. At the very end, all the comics would get up onstage together and dive right into a Wildstyle rap battle. I was gonna be the youngest comic up there by far, probably the only white dude, and I knew I'd have a target painted right on my pale, skinny back.

If doing stand-up in Gary's empty club while he hurled tennis balls at my face was a mindfuck, this audition was gonna be a whole other level of insanity.

But you know what? I was feeling pretty good about my chances. Which shows you just how insanely young and naïve I was at the time. I so desperately wanted to believe my own hype. I so badly wanted to be the child prodigy that everyone hoped I could be. I knew Gary had taken this huge gamble on me—not just with my job that summer, but by getting his boy Nick Cannon to give me a shot in the first place. I even had my mom and my very first girlfriend drive down with me to attend the audition. That's right—the Girl with the Never Say Never Tramp Stamp. Only slightly less exotic than a dragon tattoo. I wasn't being cocky—at least no more than usual—I just wanted to show all these people who believed in me that their faith was paying off.

Well, you can imagine what happened. I'm not gonna say I got devoured by the older comics I was trying out with. I didn't embarrass myself. But nothing I said broke through. In an audition, doing stand-up—you can sense when you connect with your audience. You can hear when you land a huge laugh. It didn't happen.

I went back to Ohio with my mom and girlfriend and waited anxiously for a call that never came. Instead it was just a text from Gary saying it didn't work out. I felt sad, I felt humiliated, and honestly, after I'd moved to Los Angeles, it hadn't gone much better.

The closest thing I got to a break came with a show that never even aired. I'd landed a spot on the legendary stand-up strip *Comic-View* on BET. It was my television debut. It also filmed, funny enough, in Atlanta. And the morning of the recording I got a text from Ohio telling me that my very first dog had just died. No joke—my goddamn dog died! A twelve-year-old, adorable beagle-lab mix who'd spent my whole childhood curled up next to me in my bed, practically the only wholesome memory I had—and she literally died the morning of my set.

My life was basically a shitty country music song, but I fucking hated country music. I got all dressed up like Macklemore in my Jeremy Scott winged Adidas—if you don't know the shoes I'm talking about, please google them because they literally have these ridiculous big-ass wings—I went up in front of an all-Black crowd, and I got a motherfucking standing ovation.

But no one—including me—ever saw it on TV. Because before my episode even aired, the show got canceled. Off BET. That, my friends, is failing to clear a very, very low bar.

I did get one good thing out of it, though. I ended up becoming good buddies with the show's casting director, Amber Bickham, who had "discovered me" one night when I went up at a prominent Black club in Los Angeles called the Comedy Union. Granted, she discovered me for a show that didn't even make the cut on BET. But she discovered me, briefly, nonetheless.

A few months later, Amber did me an even bigger favor. The biggest straight-up favor anyone had ever done for me. She gave me my very first car.

You read that right. She *gave me* my very first car.

I was still doing my usual routine of getting to the bus stop an hour early, hoping it would show, then riding along as homeless dudes relieved themselves around me, when one random afternoon I got a call from Amber.

"Matt," she said, "I have been so blessed in my life in so many ways, and now I want to bless you. I just bought myself a new car, and now I'd like you to have my old car. Will you accept it?"

Fuck yeah, I'd accept it!

I was so tired of taking the bus everywhere. Now I'd be able to cruise around town in my brand-new, uh . . . 2003 white Honda Civic. Okay, maybe not *exactly* brand-new. But what the hell did I care? It was my own set of wheels! I was gonna be fucking Matt "Road Warrior" Rife on the mean streets of LA!

And then, three months later, on those very same mean streets of LA, I was driving down the highway when suddenly smoke started pouring out from under the hood.

"What the hell?"

I had no fucking idea what to do. I'd never even owned a car before, much less one that looked like it was about to explode. I turned the wheel, swerved off the road, and pulled right into the nearest completely unreputable auto mechanic.

He popped the hood and whistled. "Boss, you are lucky this whole thing didn't burst into flames. This car is done."

So much for Matt "Road Warrior" Rife.

As far as my career went, I felt like I just couldn't get a break—even when people were *trying* to be nice to me. And most of the time in LA it didn't even feel like I was getting that. I was running on empty. Which I guess was at least better than having my engine explode.

I landed a couple guest star roles on some programs for Disney XD, which was like an offshoot of the Disney Channel focused on preteens. The fact that I still hadn't hit puberty looked like it was finally working in my favor, but the gigs never went anywhere, so I was back to my beardless existence without even a job to show for it.

Then I got a second shot at a spot on my dream show. Cast members Mikey Day and Pete Davidson had just got called up to the Majors and were graduating from the show, so *Wild 'N Out* needed a couple new white guys to round things out. And I mean that literally—at the time, the show's cast was almost entirely male and almost entirely Black. They liked to have at least one white dude around just to make, well . . . white-guy jokes.

Gary had to seriously beg Nick Cannon to give me another shot. I honestly can't blame Nick for being skeptical—I had flamed out only two years earlier. Why would I be any different this time? But Gary insisted that I had grown. And I literally had. Just barely. I was almost twenty years old, and puberty was finally—finally— just starting to set in. I had also grown as a comic, in experience and in confidence, or at least I felt like I had. And, you know, I also had the whole white thing down, more or less.

I flew myself back to Atlanta on my own dime to audition for the show in Gary's brand-new club, the Atlanta Comedy Theater. This time I didn't call in my mom or my Ex with the Never Say Never Tattoo. But honestly, the results were pretty much the same.

Just like two years prior, none of my best jokes had really landed. I hadn't connected with Nick Cannon and the other judges on the panel. I'd gotten what most people only dream of—a second shot at achieving my biggest dream—and I fucking blew it.

By early 2015, I was running out of options, I was running out of money, and I was running out of hope. So I grabbed on to the one lifeline anyone in Hollywood seemed willing to throw me.

A job bagging groceries, so generously offered to me by a random lady at Ralphs.

Hallelujah.

It was the weekend before my miraculous bagging job at Ralphs was set to begin, and I was at Gary's house in Atlanta.

I was in town to work his club for a week or so. Which is saying something when you think about it—I'd been living in Los Angeles for a couple years, yet in some ways Atlanta still felt like my natural creative home. The only thing Georgia seemed to lack at this point was a supermarket that would offer me a primetime gig at checkout.

Then, out of nowhere, I got a call on my cell. First thing I thought was who the hell calls people anymore? Can't you just text me like a civilized human being? But the second thing I thought was . . . hold up. What's this number? California?

I answered the phone, and it was the casting director from *Wild 'N Out*. I had gotten the job. Looks like I had made a connection after all.

Gary's whole household erupted in cheers. Hugs and high fives all around. Gary is a big fan of cigars for a big celebration, but I think they're disgusting. I'm so used to smoking weed—where you vacuum up every ounce of smoke like a human Hoover—that the whole idea of *not* inhaling makes no sense to me. The one time I tried smoking a cigar a few years back, I sucked in one puff and I wanted to fucking vomit.

But I didn't need to smoke anything to feel the buzz of this news. It was crazy. Just a few minutes ago, I was doubting the whole course of my life. Now, one call later, it felt like the entire world was mine.

There was just one thing I had to do. I got on my phone and googled the Hollywood Ralphs.

"Yeah, hey," I said when someone picked up. "I just wanted to let y'all know that I won't be coming in for training this week. Something just came up."

"That's cool," the dude on the other end said. "It'll always be here if you need it."

I damn well hoped I never did.

9

WILD 'N WHITE GUY

Before there was a single taping of *Wild 'N Out*, before I was in a single episode, there was workshop. The entire cast getting together to compete for depth chart positions really, try out material, test out games, and, you know, just kind of get comfortable with each other.

"RIFE! Where's your fuckin' head at right now?"

So much for getting comfortable.

The dude yelling at me was Nile Evans, the show's executive producer. This guy is an entertainment and comedy genius—but he looks like the scariest damn security guard you've ever seen in your life. He runs about six foot six, 280 pounds, with a thick black beard, a black hat, and a deep, powerful voice. When he yells at you, you hear it. And right now, he was definitely yelling at me.

"Getcho fuckin' hands out of your pockets and stand up straight like a man!"

Was I a man? I thought so, last time I checked, anyway. But Nile was dead-on. I had walked onto set carrying myself like a loser. I was every bit of five foot eleven, 138 pounds of pure bitch. I slouched everywhere I went. Hands in my pockets, shoulders rounded, concave chest. Even when I was doing stand-up, I'd stand with my arms crossed, kinda looking at the mic.

Nile grabbed me, pulled me in front of everyone. *Shit.*

"You know our show, dawg! Everyone will be literally trying to grab the microphone out of your hands! You gotta carry yourself, you gotta be ready! What if someone presses you?"

See, what you gotta understand is that even though I'd gotten past my audition, on *Wild 'N Out*, the competition was just getting started. The show has access to a thirty-person roster of comics—and only fourteen slots to fill per episode. That meant that each week, each show, you were fighting for your life.

And the guys I was competing against? These were all grown men! They had children, they had beards, and they all had experience in this realm. I'd even heard that a few of them had police records for shit like possession of drugs and guns. What did I have? I had a face and back covered with zits because at the age of nineteen I was finally—finally—just barely starting puberty. And the only "police record" I had was from pantsing a frenemy of mine back in high school. Pantsing a kid! He complained to his parents, so they actually pressed charges, took me to court, where the judge rolled his eyes and was like, "Seriously? You're here because you pantsed someone?" Thank God I didn't accidentally grab any of his underwear—they would've tried to give me the chair. The closest I'd been to jail was sleeping on a guy's couch in Atlanta.

This was my street cred. And now I was supposed to fight for airtime with—

"Yo, D.C.! D.C., go on and press this dude!"

And suddenly D.C. Young Fly was in my face.

D.C. Young Fly was built like one of the worm aliens from *Men in Black*. He was just as skinny as me, if not skinnier, he was a few inches taller, he had *DC* tatted right between his eyes, he was a straight-up Westside of ATL gangsta who absolutely reeked of overconfidence, and now he was standing chest-to-chest with me, grabbing my shirt, staring me dead in the eyes.

Did I think he was gonna swing on me? No. But the combative energy was there, and it was real. I tried to hold my own, tried to stare back without flinching, without anyone noticing the way my hands were shaking. But I just wasn't there yet.

"So?" Nile shouted. "*You ready for this?*"

If I thought I was, I'd never been more wrong in my fucking life.

Somehow, I managed to earn one of the fourteen spots in the very first show of the season, taping the week after the infamous workshop. Who knows—maybe they just needed a white guy that bad.

Even though I made the cut, the competition was far from over. Not only did I have to fight to get a line in one of the games, but I had to come strong. If what I said wasn't funny enough, they'd simply edit it—and me—out of the episode. It'd be like I was never even there. And honestly, exposure was really the only reason for doing *Wild 'N Out*.

The pay? A measly thousand dollars per episode—*if* you made the episode. You heard that right. A thousand bucks to be on TV. So much for Hollywood riches, right? I'd probably be making more bagging groceries at Ralphs. If I wanted to make this pay off, I needed to get that airtime. I needed to use this show as a springboard to something bigger and better, just like Kevin Hart and Pete Davidson and the others had before me.

Plus, the episode's guest team captain was none other than Shaq—not only one of the most dominant NBA big men of all time, but also a huge media personality in his own right.

You know. No pressure.

The filming got started, and I waited for what felt like forever to get a chance to say or do something—anything—to get noticed. And then it arrived. The game was called "Flo Job," and my task was simple enough. I had to go out and freestyle rap a joke, and then the other comics had to guess my imaginary "job."

Easy, right? After all, I rapped along to my favorite songs all the time. This time I'd just be using my own words. Nothing to worry about.

I walked to the middle of the stage—and then I stopped. I'd never realized just how *exposed* I was out in front of everyone. In stand-up, even in the biggest arenas in the world, the lights are so bright and the theater is so dark that the most you can see are the front five or six rows. You're really performing for the darkness.

But now I could see everything. The studio audience of over a hundred people, the fifty-person crew, the director, the cameramen, the sound guys, the producers, the other comics—everyone staring at me, watching me, waiting for me to begin. And then something happened.

For the first time in my life, I had an anxiety attack.

My hands went corpse cold. I tried to talk, and I couldn't. I tried to swallow, but my mouth was too dry. My brain was flipping out—WHAT THE FUCK IS GOING ON??—but I had no idea, because nothing like this had ever happened before.

It probably only lasted a second, but to me it felt like forever. Finally I managed to get my line out, but I mangled it. As an interesting aside to other aspiring white guys out there—freestyle rapping is actually a lot harder than rapping to a song you already know. You've got to figure out your own cadence, your own beat, and you have to do this while being, well, white. If you lean into the awkwardness, really own how bad you are, it can actually be pretty funny. But if you don't, something like this happens:

"Sitcho ass down, white boy!" they shouted—and this was my *own team*!

The buzzer *buzzed*, and that's exactly what I did—I sat my ass down. I was basically moments from getting booted off the show before I really even got my start. That's not an exaggeration. A few bad outings and the producers will straight-up cut your ass. Why waste their time on a comic who can't produce?

And I had basically no time to recover from the first nightmare before the pressure was on again. Because they shot two episodes every day.

I had to get my shit together. Had to.

Before the next episode started shooting, I thought of everything I'd been through to get to this moment. I thought of Grandpa Steve buying enough tickets to get me a spot performing in a shitty open mic in Ohio. I thought of Gary bringing me down for my summer in Atlanta. Hell, I even thought of him trying to peg me in the nuts with tennis balls. *Thwap! Thwap!* And of course I thought of Nile yelling at me to get my hands out of my pockets, stand up straight, and be a fucking man.

So that's what I did. I pulled my shoulders back, I stood up straight as a rod, I balled my hands into fists, and then relaxed them, getting loose. And I went out there and performed. Guess who I went up against in the final Wildstyle rap battle?

None other than D.C. Young Fly. But this time I was ready.

"All right, D.C.—we can just do this, I don't need a build-up. Why you look like the bad guy from *Captain Phillips*?"

D.C. got up in my face, Nick Cannon grabbing his shirt like he was holding him back. "I never seen that show and no cop y'all. Before this show, your whole family—I would've robbed y'all."

The crowd cheered, but now I was ready to drop my bomb. "You're always on the Black Squad, no matter whats. I think the scar on your face is from Nick Cannon's nuts."

Everyone went fucking *crazy*. But of course D.C. wasn't done: "I ain't cool, sho ain't your friend. Your family's so sweet, I robbed y'all again!"

It was a sick line. But nothing was gonna top Nick Cannon's nuts. Literally, figuratively, you name it. D.C. and I went back and forth relentlessly like that all season, leveling each other up. In a weird way, we actually had a chemistry I didn't have with anyone else. There was something about his crazy confidence that was infectious. I fed off it, gave it right back.

When I first got airtime on *Wild 'N Out*, I couldn't believe the response. My social media was at about twenty thousand followers, but suddenly I started adding hundreds a day—an incredible number for me back then. "Who this new white boy?" people said. "He funny as hell!"

Shit. Maybe being Token White Dude wasn't so bad after all.

An Open Letter to Zendaya

Dear Miss Zendaya (is Miss too formal? I wanna get off to a good first—I mean second—start),

Did it mean as much to you as it did to me?

All right, all right. I know this happened, like, what—ten or twenty years ago? Something like that? And I know it was literally just a three-second exchange on a completely fake TV show where I was literally supposed to do something ridiculous to make you laugh, but I wanted you to know that that was a really, really special moment for me.

At least that's what the internet says. And the internet is always right, so it must be true, so I must have been totally, definitely, absolutely shooting my shot and hitting on you that day in front of a bunch of TV cameras, the other comics, and over a hundred people in the crowd. Definitely.

And I'll admit it, all right? Maybe we got off to a little bit of a bumpy start. Maybe I didn't exactly bring my A-material that day. But can you blame me? After all, you were my teen crush, and I was truly and desperately trying to win your heart—I swear I've seen that a million times on Twitter and TikTok, so it is 100 percent true—that I just couldn't handle the pressure. But I was still a kid! Just nineteen! We're both older now, both wiser, both very private people who are never at all in the public eye.

Let's give this another shot, aight? After entirely embarrassing myself the first time, this time will be better, I swear. More personal. More heartfelt. More authentic. I'll make absolutely certain there are only three TV cameras following us for our dinner date. A sound team. An intimacy coordinator. A few social media randos recording the entire thing on their cell phones.

Because I deeply, desperately, romantically believe that any-thing on TV is real, and everything the internet thinks is gospel.

Love (not really, in case you didn't pick up the sarcasm),

Matt Rife

P.S.—For the 20 percent of the people and bots who scan this and who will not *pick it up, that entire letter was one big-ass joke and I was being 1,000 percent sarcastic.*

P.P.S.—Or was I?

P.P.P.S.—YES, I WAS. JESUS! YOU PEOPLE ARE INSANE.

Over the next couple seasons of *Wild 'N Out*, I got pretty comfortable in my role as Token White Dude. I mean, having an actual job definitely came with perks.

I finally got off Cameron Abdo's couch—and on lucky nights, his bed—and into a house. Full of five strangers. Living in separate rooms. Who I met on Craigslist. Looking back, it's unclear if that was actually a step up from a couch, but it felt like progress at the time.

I even managed to find a new girlfriend. I met her on my old go-to Instagram, which was at least better than Craigslist. And she was thirty, so again she was older than me—much older. Because, bro, *everyone* has a type.

It turned out she also had a type. Because think about it, right? I might have just started lifting weights, but I was still basically this skinny little teenager with bad teeth, no real job, no money, and I'd just graduated from a couch to living with a house full of strange dudes. She, on the other hand, had short blond hair, an incredible body, and was absolutely in the sexual prime of her life. And she'd make me these incredible vegetarian breakfast tacos—so, you know, basically marriage material. A couple months after we started going out, I finally had to ask.

"Yo, so what was it about me *specifically* that got you to respond to my first DM? Like, was it because you thought I was funny? Because I had pretty eyes? What was the deal?"

"Well," she said, kinda hesitating, "you know I'm bi, right?"

"Um," I said. "Yeah. I know that."

"Well, the first time I saw your pic I just figured you were a girl."

"Oh."

"But *totally* a very cute, very, very sexy girl."

Yeah, because that *totally* made everything so much better. Needless to say, I started lifting at Crunch with Dane Cook even more to try and stop looking like a handsome lesbian.

After season one, I also finally—finally—fixed the bane of my existence, my awful, crooked, tiny Tic Tac teeth. I mean, shit, I was on TV—I had to do *something*. So I saved up every dollar and every dime and got myself veneers—on a payment plan, might I add. I was terrified to miss an installment and open my door to find the dentist waiting with a pair of pliers. For the first time in my life, I finally felt confident enough to start smiling with my lips parted.

Honestly, I think my girlfriend was more shocked to see my shiny new teeth than she was by the fact that I had a dick.

And to be clear, even though I was stuck being the white guy—because I was, you know, white—we *all* had roles to play. D.C. Young Fly, for example, is a smart, super funny, infinitely talented dude, but his role was "gangsta." That was his lane. Everyone had one.

I got into a groove, got more comfortable with the constant competition, but the job also came with some pretty blatant limitations.

If I cracked a joke about how white people always pay our taxes, how we can't dance, how we hate spicy food—you know, real groundbreaking shit—the crowd would seriously *roar* with laughter. Like this was the funniest stuff they'd ever heard in their lives. But if I ever tried anything that felt remotely clever or experimental to me—I ain't talking Picasso here, I just mean a joke that didn't somehow play off my race or age—it would be straight-up *crickets* out there. A producer would shoot me a look like, "What the fuck was that? Just do *white*." And the joke would automatically get cut from the aired episode.

And even though I felt like the rest of the cast did come to accept me, I never felt like I made any real connections with anyone on the show. These were, at best, work friends. Or you know what? It was really more like high school.

It felt like everyone else was in this special clique. They were really good bros with each other, but I was stuck on the outside.

If I just happened to catch someone by himself, if we were one-on-one, everything would be cool for a second. Like, *awesome, I got a friend! This is happening!* But the moment anyone else came around, it was like I didn't exist anymore. That's what life on *Wild 'N Out* felt like.

In a way, it all felt kind of natural to me. From almost the very beginning, it was always Black comedians and Black clubs blessing me with opportunity. In my very first days of performing at Gary's club in Atlanta, I had learned how to loosen up a mostly Black crowd by doing a goofy impression of Justin Bieber. Now, on the show, they did regular bits about me as Justin Bieber. Even growing up in Columbus, the Black community had always accepted me and blessed me with the most opportunity. Black friends and their families were always the people I was closest to. I was used to being an outsider among outsiders.

I was also used to being independent. To this day, I tend to hold my feelings in. I'm really quick with a smile and a joke, it's my natural instinct to make people feel comfortable around me. But if you want the real me? If you want to know what I really think? How I really feel? Yeah, I don't think so. I reserve that for a very special few people. Sometimes I don't share it with anyone at all.

So in a sense, being a social castoff on the show, being pigeon-holed as the white dude, none of that bothered me. But I'm also someone who's never satisfied with the status quo. I love to challenge boundaries, push the envelope—especially when it comes to comedy.

Which is how as a teenager in my very first season on the show, I managed to set the whole fucking internet on fire with the touch of someone's chin.

I mean, I assume that if you're reading this book you know who Zendaya is.

Well, back in 2015 she was still definitely Zendaya . . . but she wasn't exactly, you know, *Zendaya* quite yet. I knew her from watching her when I was in middle school and high school, when she was still a Disney star. And yeah, I absolutely had a crush on her. I was an adolescent boy—I had a crush on everyone!

But when I found out she was gonna be a Guest Team Captain on the show, I wasn't focused on any old crush I had. I was thinking that this was another great chance to break through. To win the never-ending competition on *Wild 'N Out*, yes, but even more than that—to get exposure. To get noticed and make my mark so I could move onto something even bigger.

For better or worse, I *definitely* ended up getting noticed.

The game was called "Talking Spit," which was basically one of the hardest—and least fun—games to play on the show. The whole point was for us to get Zendaya to laugh so hard that she spat out some water she had in her mouth. Now think about it. If you've ever laughed hard enough to spit out your drink—and most of us have—it usually happens because you're not expecting it. Someone makes a ridiculous joke, usually out of nowhere, and the laugh just sneaks up on you.

It usually does *not* happen when you're sitting in a chair, surrounded by cameras, expecting to hear jokes, and trying your hardest not to laugh at any of them.

And Zendaya, like most celebs who'd played the game, was proving impossible to break. Comic after comic brought out their best stuff, and every one of them got shot down. It was finally my turn, and my brain zoomed back to Nile shouting at me to stand up straight, shoulders back, and be a fucking man. It was time to be me without apology. It was time to push some comedy boundaries with my old celebrity crush.

I strutted out like a teenage peacock, pumping every ounce of energy I had into my skinny, five-foot-eleven frame. "Fuck that!" I shouted. "I'm Matt *Mothafuckin'* Rife. You're mixed, I wanna be Black . . . let's make a Lifetime movie."

She giggled but didn't come close to a spit take. The audience chuckled, charmed, probably thinking, "Classic goofy white boy!"

I was so close to getting that laugh. So close! But I needed more. *Challenge those comic conventions, dawg! Commit to your bit!*

"Girl," I said, "spit that water out so I can get your number! *Please!*"

Then, as if I was literally in some *Romeo and Juliet* kind of way trying to woo this unattainable, untouchable lost love of mine, I, well . . . touched her. I touched Zendaya's chin. Super briefly. Like, if you watch the clip—and trust me, it's out there, so you can—it all happens so fast you can barely see it. To me it seemed like nothing.

To the rest of the world? Apparently, not so much.

The energy in the room shifted immediately. Like this weird shockwave of *He touched Zendaya's chin! He touched Zendaya's chin!* And someone from the other team, trying to hijack the game, shouted, "Don't touch her! She's too young!"

My team tried to rally. Kind of. "They're the same age!" someone shouted. Which was basically true. She was eighteen and I was nineteen.

And then the killer. "Still, he got acne and his fingernails are dirty!"

Excuse me while I take a bath with my toaster.

The most brutal part of the whole thing was that they were right—under all my makeup I really did have acne. Bad. It was the glorious first sign of my long-awaited puberty, and now it was being used against me. Though to be fair, my fingernails were in fact meticulous.

Thanks to the power of the internet and the magic of MTV's incessant reruns, that single brief moment quickly took on a life of its own. It amounted to one of the most viral incidents of the entire season, maybe in the history of the show. Two years later, the show posted the scene on YouTube—along with very, um, insightful commentary—and that's gone over 26 million views. How many of those clicks came after my career took off? Damned if I know. But what I do know is that when it actually happened, it felt like the whole world was in an uproar.

And my initial response was: *Wait, what? This was a bit. On a TV show. Everyone knows this was a bit, right? How can they possibly not know it was a bit?*

Well, Matt, welcome to your first taste of internet logic. Where a TikTok challenge tells women to superglue their lips to create a better pout—and apparently, I really was trying to seduce Zendaya up on that stage.

After four seasons, I decided to leave *Wild 'N Out*. I was stalling creatively as the Token White Guy, and at a thousand bucks an episode it's not like I was getting rich. I had accomplished what I set out to do. I gained confidence, I learned how to carry myself in front of an audience, think quick on my feet, and most important of all I got incredible national exposure. Not all of it the good kind.

The acne is gone. But the YouTube video is not. To this day, people will come up to me and seriously ask, "Did you get her number?"

Nope. Nor did I ever ask.

10

MERRY SUMO CHRISTMAS

I was in the middle of a shoot in the heart of the iconic Times Square. Surrounded by gleaming glass buildings and cameras and producers and everything that made New York so special—all the lights, all the tourists, all the shops and hustlers and street performers and just the beautiful teeming chaos of it all.

And in so, *so* many ways, I was living my fucking dream.

It was 2017, just a few months after I left *Wild 'N Out*, and the show was a reboot of another MTV classic, *TRL*, the '90s hit series that defined music and culture for an entire generation. I was getting paid to be one of the hosts—and when I say paid, I mean *paid*. I was making more money in a week than my parents saw in a year.

Not only would I finally be able to afford to move out of my awkward Craigslist house, but when we filmed the show in NYC, the network put me up in the penthouse—the penthouse!—of this massive high-rise right by where the ball dropped on New Year's Eve. Just a short while ago, my "bedroom" in LA had walls made of IKEA bookshelves. Now my walk-in closets had walk-in closets.

Back in LA I'd taken the bus with homeless dudes, or at best I drove a free used car that almost turned into a fireball on the expressway. Now, MTV wouldn't even let me pay for a cab. It was nothing but a black chauffeured SUV from here on out. Me? Walk somewhere? Hell no—I wanted all my transportation bullet-proofed.

But in so many other ways, I totally was not.

Half the reason I'd left *Wild 'N Out*—other than the fact that they barely paid anyway—was because I wanted to grow as a comic. I wanted to try new things, get out of the Token White Guy business, push myself on the stage and as an actor. When MTV called me about co-hosting *TRL*, they had guaranteed that I'd get to write and perform some of my own material, that the show would feature sketch comedy, and especially, *especially* . . .

"Guys, respectfully, I have zero interest in interviewing a bunch of Vine and TikTok kids. That shit makes me want to puke. Respectfully. None of that."

Now here I was. I'd been hosting the show for four months, and I was making more money than I'd ever dreamed. But I was working twelve-hour days, from seven a.m. to seven p.m., so there was no time for me to do stand-up. I was in New York for a minimum of five days out of the week, so my LA comedy connections were starting to assume I had given up or was out of the game. On the show, I never got to write my own stuff, and we definitely never did any sketches. Other than the money, it was the exact opposite of everything I wanted.

"All right!" the assistant director shouted. "Everyone to their places!"

I sighed, shuffled over to my spot on set, and turned my head. I was staring right at one of the giant mirrored windows of a Times Square skyscraper. Right at my own reflection.

I was dressed in a black-and-white-striped referee's costume, and I was standing between two Vine kids who were wearing those ridiculous fat, plastic sumo costumes you can find at any two-bit carnival. I was about to ref "The Vine Sumo Battle of the Century."

What the fuck am I doing? I thought.

Honestly, I had no idea. But I did know what I was *gonna* do. For the first time in my life, I had realized that as much as it sucks to be poor—and it does suck, I can tell you that from experience— money would not buy me happiness.

The very next day, I quit the fucking show. It got canceled two weeks later. Given all the hype, the *TRL* reboot remains one of the most notorious flops in MTV history.

Hold The Applause.

It was almost Christmas, and I decided that for once, instead of going back home, I'd stay in LA and do a friends Christmas—I don't know, I've heard of Friendsgiving, so maybe this is Friends-mas? Christbros? Whatever it was, I was doing it.

Even though I'd been out of the Midwest for years at this point, I still don't love it to this day. What am I supposed to feel nostal-gic about? Oh yeah, that dusty old gas station and pizza joint—so quaint. Being called a "faggot loser" and getting cut from the freshman basketball team? (To be clear, those weren't the coach's words—he said something worse.) Naw, I've pretty much had enough of that for a lifetime.

And my relationship with my parents was . . . complicated. I love my mom like crazy; I know she's always trying her hardest for me and my sister. I mean, this is someone who started out as a single mom, then got trapped in a shitty marriage, but still man-aged to support me in the best ways she knew how. Letting me leave home at a young age to go to Atlanta and then Los Angeles. Driving out to support me at some of my biggest auditions and tapings—even if they usually didn't go anywhere. I don't fault her for all the shit I experienced with my abusive stepdad. For the way I felt like a stranger in my own home for so much of my childhood. We were all making the best of a situation that was tough as shit.

But still—emotions are weird, you know? People are weird. I'm weird. We're all fucking weird. I'm not ashamed to say that I'm still trying to sort through all this garbage in therapy to this day.

This was also right around when puberty, after taking its sweet time for more than twenty years, finally decided to hit me square in the face. Over a few months, I went from looking like a thirteen-year-old to looking like, you know, my actual age. Like an actual grown-ish man. My face got wider, my features became more prominent, I grew a few inches taller. Working out at the gym, which had started as a fun way to hang with Dane Cook, became a kind of therapy in its own right. I started every day off by lifting. It cleared my head, got me in the right mindset, helped me feel positive. And I still fucking hated doing legs, because only psychos like to do legs. So my body, my entire frame got bigger, too.

And just like that, my bizarrely stunted journey through puberty became the basis for about a million-and-one internet conspiracies about all this elaborate plastic surgery I somehow had the time and money to undergo.

Straight up—if you are an actual doctor actually going on TikTok to proclaim a guaranteed diagnosis about a dude you've never even *met* before, much less treated, how the hell do you not lose your license? At the very least for a frightening lack of common sense. Can the medical board please just issue an official certificate telling you to get a life? *Something* to help these people get their priorities straight, because they desperately need it.

All of a sudden, thanks to the same diabolical magic that has given growing boys deeper voices and hair on their balls, I was good-looking. And I was like—*whoa*, I guess good-looking people don't always have it easy! If anything, as a comedian, it actually made shit harder! And if you don't believe me, think about why that statement bothered you, and you prove my point. Judgment.

As a comic you're supposed to make the audience like you, right? Well, who the fuck likes attractive people? No one! Hell, for the first twenty-two years of my life I hated them, too. You just assume they've always gotten everything in life handed to them on a silver platter. There's no sympathy for pretty people at all. No support groups for Fuckboys Anonymous (patent pending).

But it turns out that pretty people are fucked-up, too. Who knew? I'm in therapy. I've had multiple anxiety attacks. I struggle with clinical depression, and I have complicated feelings about life, about my mom, about loneliness.

There's pretty much only one family member who ever made things feel completely simple for me, and that was Grandpa Steve. My papaw. He'd always been who I turned to, he'd always been my best friend growing up, he drove me to my very first open mics in Columbus, so I decided to invite him out to Los Angeles to join us for Christmas.

Papaw had been talking forever about visiting me on the West Coast. This guy would even go on and on about how he wanted to move here. Seriously, my grandpa Steve living in Hollywood! I mean, I love the dude, so I actually looked around to see if there was a place he could afford. There wasn't. But besides that, the idea of this old-timer who bitched about traffic in *small town Ohio* trying to navigate the utter shit show of LA streets was ridiculous. I could just hear him trying to carry a conversation while he tried to drive his pickup truck through bumper-to-bumper cars on the Sunset Strip.

"So I—*fucking cut me off!*—was just wondering—*goddamn out of nowhere!!*—if maybe we should go—*dickweed!!!*—maybe just— *check your fucking blind spot, asshole!*—get lunch now—*yeah, you speed motherfucker, cops are waitin'!!!! FUCK!!*—or somethin'."

But a Christmas visit? That was another matter. I told him I would cover it, so he didn't have any excuses to back out. My man lived by himself, he didn't have many friends, he barely got out of the house—hell, he hadn't even flown on a plane for at least a few decades. I figured a little adventure would do him good. Most of all, since he was my real family, I thought it would be nice to have him out to finally visit my brand-new family in Los Angeles.

I'm a big believer in that old saying that friends are the family you get to choose. It might be a cliché, but it's a cliché for a reason. I didn't really have a dad, I didn't have any brothers, so instead I chose a bunch of people to fill those gaps once I got to Los Angeles. But we all kind of do that, don't we? Y'all know what I'm talking about.

You have a friend you can always rely on and go to for advice— for me that was Erik Griffin, the dude who first welcomed me to LA. You have a friend who *never shuts the fuck up*—and don't act like you don't! We all do! For me, that's my buddy Alex. Alex opens for me on my tours to this day, and I love the dude. But this motherfucker has no off switch.

And he's just *loud*. I mean irresponsibly loud. His whisper is a foghorn. But Alex also has a lot of great qualities. Which means you can straight-up tell him, "Hey dude, you sound like a dumbass right now. Please. Shut. Up," and he accepts it. He takes it. And then he keeps on talking anyway.

Then of course you got your twin. The guy you just click with. Like you always have fun together, you're on the exact frequency no matter what. The best friend.

Now, I just want to start out by saying this is all gonna sound gay as fuck. I acknowledge that, I understand that, and I accept that. Now let's get past it, all right?

A few years earlier, I'd met this dude at a Christmas party—I *told* you, gay as fuck!—and it wasn't just any Christmas party. It was a Christmas party being thrown by the commercial agent of another very good buddy of mine, Kevin (he's the friend you have who flakes the most, but you'd die for—sorry, Kevin). Remember what I told you about auditioning for commercials? It's like acting on crack, just completely over the top and ridiculous and disgusting.

Well, this was a Christmas party held by a commercial agent, so a dude who just trafficked in all that shit. Kind of like if Satan celebrated the holidays. A gay Krampus, if you will. This was at a club, there was a DJ, a dance floor, free drinks and food—it should've been fun, but it was very entertainment-industry oriented, so it was actually very stuffy. We're talking shiny gray suits, everyone networking, everyone stiff, everyone tight.

Well, I was standing there, bored as shit, when suddenly the DJ tossed on Cali Swag District's "Teach Me How to Dougie," so I charged out onto the dance floor and—what else?—I hit the

Dougie. In case you aren't aware, the Dougie is an absurdly popular dance, and if you don't know how to do it, go grab your SPF 7000 you Caucasian relic.

I'm out there, dancing by myself, not giving a shit, when suddenly I see this other dude out there with me, and like the very best meet-cute out of the very gayest rom-com—I tossed a dance move off to him. He did a few steps, then he tossed it back to me.

That was how I met James.

This dude laughed the same as me, he had the same sense of humor as me. It was impossible for us to not have a good time around each other. James became the core of my new family of friends in Los Angeles. He played the role of the friend who's always fun to be around, while I played the role of the friend who's the responsible one. That's right—the responsible one. Which tells you something about just how fucked-up my friends are.

And this is exactly what my grandpa Steve was walking into over the holidays.

Papaw did LA the way only Papaw could. This man who hadn't been on a plane in literally dozens of years got on his flight with only a flip phone—no iPod, no computer, not even a book—and he just sat there, staring straight ahead, raw dogging the flight for six straight hours. Just lost in his thoughts. Or maybe thinking of nothing at all. Who knows how that brain worked.

When he got to our place, I showed him the technological marvel that is streaming for the very first time. "Papaw, I got Netflix, I got Hulu—you can watch any single show you've ever dreamed of watching. Right here. Right now."

My guy selected *The Ranch*, a sitcom starring Ashton Kutcher and Sam Elliot. Two great actors, but still—*The Ranch*?

I took him down to the Santa Monica Pier to see the Pacific Ocean for the first time in his life, and I said, "Papaw, LA has some of the best food in the world. Restaurants of every kind, from every chef, from every country. Tell me where you want to go and it's yours."

He picked Bubba Gump Shrimp. I'm not gonna pretend there's anything great about that one. Maybe the trivia. Like, what was the name of Forrest's school bus driver?

Dorothy Harris, people. Get it together, ya boy's a movie buff.

On Christmas Eve I literally begged the man, "Please, *please*, let me take you somewhere special tonight. PLEASE."

He looks at me and goes, "Is there an Olive Garden around?"

I said, "*What?*"

He shrugged. "It's my favorite restaurant."

What could I say? If someone had asked me the same thing, I probably would've asked for McDonald's.

But when Christmas Day finally arrived, it was fucking glorious. It was me and Grandpa Steve and all my LA friends. My buddies got me and Papaw matching pajamas, which we promptly put on. Whatever my grandpa's taste in restaurants, he was an amazing cook. He spent hours making ham, cheesy potatoes, green beans, and stuffing—which he insisted on calling "dressing," which always drove me crazy. People, you put dressing on *salads*, all right? That's what dressing is, and it is *not* the same thing as stuffing. One of them is delicious, and the other is drizzle. I'm as trash as they come, and even I know that. Jesus!

While he cooked, the rest of us sat around our little plastic tree, watched old Christmas movies—no *Bad Santa*, unfortunately, because even we weren't that crass—and pretty much just smoked weed all day—because, okay, I guess we were that crass.

The weed didn't bother Papaw at all. He'd smoked his fair share back in the seventies, when he first grew out his long-ass ponytail, but back then it was a different drug altogether, a ton weaker. Probably half seeds, half oregano, and none of the fancy growing science they use today. I got him a weed pen once. He took a hit, got real quiet, and just went, "Oh yeah. Oh yeah, I can feel that."

Like, "Yeah, Papaw, maybe your hair hasn't changed—but herb definitely has. This strain is literally called *The Devil's Foreskin*."

At the end of his trip, Grandpa Steve flew back to Ohio feeling kinda like a new man. Maybe he'd never move to LA—I don't think the highways could've handled that—but he decided to start getting out more. I helped him get online, made him a Facebook account, and he even started reconnecting with a few people from high school. Papaw was finally getting out of his shell.

And me? After a few years living in Los Angeles, trying to get myself and my career established, it was finally starting to feel like home. I was getting emotional support from my family and from my family of friends. And I felt like for the first time in years I was back to pursuing my career in entertainment on my own terms, not the terms of some random network or TV show.

There was just one problem. Doing things on my own terms wasn't great when it came to paying my bills.

From my four-month stint on the *TRL* reboot, I'd managed to save up a little nest egg of about fifty grand. Which actually felt like a shit ton of money to a guy who'd spent the last few years sleeping on a couch and taking the city bus.

I was like, "Yes! I'm fucking rich!" And then, like the financial genius I was, I acted like it. Upgraded my wardrobe. Moved into that apartment with the actual room. Took a few little trips with my best friend James to Mexico, to Ireland, to New Orleans, to Hawaii. Okay, maybe more than a few little trips. And I bought myself a brand-new Jeep Wrangler. That cost me about forty grand. Then I filled up its massive gas tank, and that cost me another forty grand. It's amazing how fast a twenty-three-year-old kid can blow through a few thousand bucks.

By 2019 I was back to being pretty much broke.

But if you're a comic, even when you're on your last few pennies, you still gotta travel. Touring is our lifeblood—even if by "touring" you mean getting up onstage in front of ten or twenty people in Wichita, Kansas. As a comic, you have to circulate, you have to be out there, you have to show face. Otherwise people just forget you exist. Audiences, booking agents, other comics—after a few weeks off the scene, it can be like you were never even there.

So that winter I went back to New York for the first time since I quit the reboot of *TRL*. My goal was simple: get up on a few comedy stages and make enough money so I'd at least break even after expenses.

That meant keeping my expenses as ridiculously low as possible. I landed at the airport on my budget flight. I trudged outside, bundled up against the cold, dragging along my giant suitcase. I lugged it onto the subway for a two-hour trip to Manhattan, which would've taken thirty minutes by cab, but who the hell could afford a cab? Finally, I got off at my stop, then dragged my suitcase up the thirty steps to the surface.

I lugged my bag out into freezing, whorling snow, sweat pouring down my back underneath my winter coat, and I looked up. There, right in front of me, was the luxury high-rise where MTV used to put me up, where their black SUV would drop me off and a driver would carry my luggage to the front. A block away was the hostel where I'd be staying this time.

Fuck. Had I come a long way? Or not very far at all? Or maybe I'd just walked backwards for a thousand fucking miles, dragging this goddamn suitcase? And why the hell did I pack so much in the first place?

Note to self: Pack less when taking the subway and sleeping in a hostel.

I got to the place I'd be staying at, and for the first time in my life I found myself wishing I was sleeping on a couch instead. The window in the dorm room was broken, so the cold winter air swirled in all night long right above the steaming, clanking radiator.

I reached the top of a bunk bed—which I guess counts as luxury in a hostel—and the dude below me had no legs. He sat there at the edge of his mattress and stared at me as I tried, and generally failed, to toss my suitcase onto my mattress.

"Hey, my man," I said, trying my best to be friendly. "Looks like we're gonna be bunkmates. My name is Matt. Pleasure to meet you."

He shook my hand, and then he said something that was most definitely not in English. I'm no expert in linguistics, but it also sounded a lot more complicated than "Hello there!"

"Um," I said. "Uh . . . no hablo . . . um . . ."

He started chattering away again, even faster now—which totally helped me understand him better—getting more and more excited as I got more and more confused.

"Uh," I said. "No . . . parlez vous . . . um . . ."

Then finally he went to the hand gestures. Pointing at his wheelchair, pointing at his legs—well, really his stumps if we're being honest here—and then pointing towards the area of his body that I can only describe scientifically as his dick and his ass.

"Oh!" I said. "You need to use the bathroom?"

This was really more of a statement than a question—I really hoped he only needed to use the bathroom, and nothing else that might involve me and his dick or his butthole—but he nodded very enthusiastically. I helped him to his chair, but I wasn't gonna wipe.

Yeah. For the rest of my stay in New York, the snow poured in our broken window, and I helped my legless bunkmate in and out of his bed, over to his wheelchair, and back over to our bathroom as we communicated with the most basic caveman sign language you can imagine and I prayed to Jesus that my roomie never needed my help with any other bodily functions. I survived the trip on street meat (mobile food vendors, not cock) and 7-Eleven, popped around the city by subway from gig to gig, and made just enough to pay for my trip, all in the name of comedy.

And I learned a new lesson to add to my original thought that money would not buy me happiness: maybe it wouldn't, but money was still a very, very nice thing to have. If I ever managed to have any money again, no matter how unhappy I might be, I was gonna appreciate that shit.

11

LOWKEY UPSET

It was March of 2020, and me and a buddy were driving from LA down to San Diego so I could headline a little show that night. You heard right—headline.

After the disaster that was *TRL* a few years earlier, my career was finally starting to pick back up. I mean, I still wasn't exactly raking in the cash, but a couple months ago I had appeared on this weird comedy contest on NBC called *Bring the Funny*. It was judged by Kenan Thompson, Chrissy Teigen, and Jeff Foxworthy, so these were legitimate people, but I wasn't just competing against other stand-ups. I was going against ventriloquists, against sketch-groups, against literal clowns—and you know what? I got to the semifinals. Fuck off, Bozo. Chrissy Teigen thinks I'm funnier than a rainbow wig and floppy shoes.

And she's ten years older than me. Could do a hell of a lot worse.

It wasn't much, but it was a boost. Suddenly clubs that had been barely interested in me were excited to put me on as the main act. I'd even been able to start booking a tour. I had ten cities lined up already, which wasn't exactly huge, but I was moving tickets; there was real momentum. Hell, Grandpa Steve even had an iPhone now. If my papaw was (nearly) done thinking computers made everybody gay, you know shit was starting to look up.

Then me and my friend turned on the car radio and heard the news: "... *due to the rapid spread of COVID, local authorities are recommending that the public begin quarantining starting tomorrow* ..."

Note to self: Never listen to the fucking news.

At first I honestly tried to brush it off. Think about it—until just a few days earlier, the government had been insisting everything would be fine as long as we sang "Happy Birthday" while washing our hands. To be fair, even that was scary to a bunch of people. But my main reaction had been ... *Hold up a second. You dudes think "Happy Birthday" is* **too long** *to wash your hands?? Have you ever taken a good look at public bathrooms? Hell, have you looked at your own bathrooms? This shit is literally disgusting!*

I've always been the kind of guy where when I wash my hands, I fucking scrub the crap out of those hands. You can call it obsessive if you want—I call it common sense. You're standing at the urinal, and I don't care how great your aim is, it's like, *Whoa, all*

132

right, there goes some splash back. Oops! Another miss—or maybe that was the guy next to me.

Then I'd head to the sink and I'd just be getting a good lather on, and some other guy who just took a dump walks over and at best like flicks a couple drops of water on his index finger—I don't even want to know what he did with his pinky—and charges right out of the bathroom and on his way. At first it was like—maybe a global pandemic isn't a bad thing if it gets y'all to practice basic hygiene, right?

But the more I listened to what this radio announcer had to say—honestly, I should really give up radio altogether and just stick to bullshit podcasts from here on out—the more worried I got. This sounded a hell of a lot more serious than whistling a merry tune and dousing my hands with Dial. "Shit," I said. "We should probably stop and pick up some groceries."

That's what we did. Or at least that's what we tried to do. I pulled into some random market on the way to the club, and everything was already starting to feel surreal. There weren't many people there, but a couple of them were already in masks, and it felt like the shelves had already been stripped bare of everything essential. Lucky I didn't need to wipe my ass. Toilet paper became precious gold if you've already forgotten.

Now, did any of this impending Armageddon make me even *remotely* consider not performing that night? Hell no! I was a professional. Plus, I needed the damn money, if only to reimburse me for the gas I was burning to drive South.

And you know what? My show was packed. Leave it to comedy fans to at least choose to go out with a smile on their face. Not only that, but a few of us comics decided to hang out after the show and make a toast to the end of the world. I had my drink at the bar and headed over to my table to grab my stuff.

"Um . . ." I said. "Hey guys? Has anyone seen my fucking jacket?"

Nope. It was gone. And so were my fucking car keys, which had been in my pocket. I didn't know whether to be depressed or inspired. On the one hand, it was like—*motherfuckers! I drive all the way to your city to make you laugh and you guys fucking rob me??* On the other hand, it was like—*wow, a mystery virus is about to destroy the entire universe, and you still have the energy to engage in petty theft. Bravo, San Diego—a real city of strivers!*

But mostly I needed to get back to Los Angeles ASAP. I had booked a part in a shitty indie film that I pray never sees the light of day, and the shoot started the next morning at eight. Me and my friend accepted our losses, closed out the bar—and because God is hilarious, it started pouring rain with nowhere to go. We were standing there getting soaked when a cute girl invited us to her house to "get our bearings"—or for a gangbang, I never found out.

My friend and I swallowed our pride, combined our bank accounts, and Ubered all the way back to LA at four in the morning. I did the shoot on no sleep, and after a twelve-hour day, my buddy drove me all the way back to San Diego with a spare key, just so I could drive my car all the way back home again.

It was annoying as hell. But I had no idea just how bad shit was about to get.

I really shoulda stuck around for that gang bang.

In a weird way, the first few weeks of lockdown were actually pretty great.

I mean, sure, life in the entire country ground to a complete halt. And yeah, a freak pandemic that maybe came from morons eating bats somehow decided to hit right as my career was finally—*finally*—starting to regain its mojo. And okay, so Grandpa Steve had to shut all his brand-new dating profiles down and would probably never get laid again. But still—vacation!

I was still living in an apartment with my buddy, right next door to Kevin and his girlfriend, who we'd just spent that amazing Christmas with—I was basically stuck inside with some of my favorite people in the world. We had the exact same routine every single day. Wake up at three in the afternoon, or maybe two if we were feeling really ambitious. Work out in the living room, using a chin-up bar, some elastic bands, and a few Bow-Flex dumbbells that Kevin owned. Smoke weed. Smoke more weed. Play *Call of Duty*. Smoke weed. Play more *Call of Duty*. Smoke more weed. Go to bed at three a.m. Wake up and smoke more weed.

That's what we called a full day. And every single day was exactly like the day before. And at first it was paradise. No work.

No responsibilities. A few checks from the government that barely covered the electricity bill. No worries. Right?

Then the panic attacks started.

I'd had the first taste of an anxiety attack back during my first taping of *Wild 'N Out*. My tongue turning to sandpaper. The palms of my hands going ice cold. Sweat covering my body. At the time, I'd never experienced anything like it. But this stuff made that anxiety attack feel like a warm, fuzzy memory.

I'd be ready to go to bed after a long day of nothing, and right out of nowhere I felt like I was having a heart attack. I mean a serious, honest heart attack. The pain flashed through my arm, then my chest. My heart pounded like a bass drum in my rib cage, except totally off rhythm, as if the drummer was a paranoid schizophrenic on coke. Then choking. I mean I seriously couldn't get any air past my throat. I'd reach up to my neck, half-expecting someone's hands to be there, squeezing.

During the day it was depression. Feeling this weird, angsty energy—constant anxiety, but also a complete inability to do anything about it. I don't know how to explain it. Somehow you both desperately want to do something but desperately do not want to do anything—all at the same time. So many feelings of self-loathing and despair and failure.

Why had I moved out to LA?

What was the point of having dreams? What was the point of anything at all?

When can I try again? Will I be able to try again?

What's normal anymore?

I tried doing my stand-up in the only way that was left to any professional comic—on Zoom. College campuses around the country still had entertainment budgets, even though they couldn't host any live shows, and they'd reach out and see if I could put on a virtual show.

"Um, sure," I'd say. "I guess?"

I'd switch on my computer and find myself staring directly at like seven college kids with oily skin and bad lighting, on mute from their dorm rooms, which was honestly better than me—I never even wore pants. I'd just sit on my couch, screen angled at my face, halfheartedly telling one gag after another. I could barely get the words out.

About five or ten minutes into my so-called set, I'd watch as one face after another vanished from the Zoom, or simply walked out of whatever student lounge they were huddled in. Usually something like that would piss me off, but now all I could think was, *Yeah, of course this sucks. Everyone in this fucking room should leave. I wish I could, too.*

Live comedy had always been my savior, my best reason for existing—I loved the physical and mental exertion, I loved the crackling energy and the uncontrolled laughter and the feeling that anything could happen at any moment—and now even that was gone.

Yeah, the pandemic was mentally and emotionally crushing. And yeah, I would think about my dad sometimes. The dude I never even knew. Well, I knew one thing—that he committed suicide. I have no idea what exactly he was going through when he decided to take his own life, but depression must've been a huge part of it. How could it not be? I also know enough science to understand that that kind of mental illness can be hereditary. My dad's brain hadn't been wired right. Something inside him snapped. Some critical part inside caused him to literally self-destruct. I had to acknowledge that some of that same darkness could be living inside me.

Thankfully, as bleak as my life became during the pandemic, I never got to the point where I wanted to end it all. Never reached that level of despair. But it was also becoming clear to me just how much of an impact my mind and my emotional state could have on my overall health. When I was depressed, when I was consumed by panic attacks, I wasn't able to function. Even if "functioning" meant waking up after noon and playing video games. I'm a sensitive fucker, to say the least.

I tried seeing a few doctors. Coincidentally, this was also around the time I decided that most doctors are morons. Doctor after doctor barely even listened to what I had to say. They wouldn't run any tests, they hardly even looked at me. They'd just puff out their chests and proclaim, "I went to medical school! *Somewhere!*" and then they'd confidently state that I seemed perfectly fine. Or they'd go in the exact opposite direction and try to put me on a bunch of brain-altering medication that I had zero interest in getting hooked on. I had no health insurance, so I had to borrow money from my friends just to do these office visits—and for what? To admire a diploma on the wall? To get pumped full of drugs?

I wasn't looking for a quick fix or a temporary patch to cover up my problems. I wanted to understand what was causing them. I wanted to get to the heart of it all. But I felt like I had no one to vent to, no one to open up to. For as much as I love Grandpa Steve and my mom, we never exactly had deep, probing conversations. Our love was more about spending time with each other, showing support through our actions. And my friends were guys I hung out with, had fun with, smoked weed and played video games with. My panic attacks, my depression, my doubts, it all felt too personal to talk to them about it. Staying guarded, staying closed off—that felt so much easier, so much safer.

I was spiraling downward. Fast. I needed to find a way out. And I did—right by my apartment's dumpster.

Paul Elia was another young comic based in LA, just like me.

His act tapped into clever but heartfelt stories about his Arab-American upbringing back in Michigan, so it wasn't surprising that he was funny as hell. What was surprising is that I didn't hate his guts for it.

Comics are notoriously competitive, and that includes me. It's not so much that you don't want the other guy or gal to be funny ... they just can't be funnier than you. It's not that comedians aren't friendly with each other—after all, you're spending almost all your time together touring or at clubs, drinking, talking, waiting to go onstage—but we don't tend to be close friends.

For me, Paul was the exception that proved the rule. He was poor and aspiring, just like me, and funny, just like me—well, maybe I was a *tiny bit* funnier—but even though we were technically competing for the same parts on the same shows and the same slots at the same clubs, I fucking loved the guy to death. Kind of like my best friend James, who I'd met on the dance floor doing the Dougie—it was a chemistry thing. We just clicked.

Paul has this undeniable positive energy. He's like a human golden retriever, always smiling, always sincere, always eager—almost to a fault. Like you could be sitting around, just chilling, and someone could say something kinda funny and just offhand go, "That could be a sketch." And Paul would be the guy who'd say "YES. Let's do it TOMORROW. I know a guy who'll shoot it, and there's sound, and the location, and the gaffing, and then of course there's the script and direction . . ." And everyone else is like, "Yeah, or we could just keep hanging out for a while."

Which is why if Paul had a role, I'd call him "the friend you'd start a pyramid scheme with."

Before the pandemic hit, that's kinda what Paul and I actually did together—a comedian's version of a pyramid scheme. Once a month we hosted our own show at the Comedy Store, in this discreet spot in the back with a members-only, exclusive vibe called the Belly Room. Running your own show pulls off a clever trifecta for an up-and-coming comic. You get a steady income—about six hundred dollars each for me and Paul—you get to build relationships in the comedy community by offering spots to friends, who then tell their friends to get a spot on your show, who then tell their friends to get on your show, and on and on. But most important, you get guaranteed stage-time and exposure yourself.

Everyone wins, baby!

We called the show "Lowkey Upset." And we ran it almost like a mini talk show. Paul and I would co-host a completely improvised opening set about anything that "upset" us, and then feature guests like Taylor Tomlinson, Ian Edwards, and of course my dawg Erik Griffin, who got to do some stand-up and then were forced to undergo a probing, hard-hitting interview from me and Paul after their set. And guess what? It fucking worked! We were getting paid, we were making important friends in the industry, we were getting our comedy out there—

And then came the fucking pandemic.

I crawled out of bed one day at the bright and early time of 3:30 p.m. The night before, I'd been destroyed by yet another panic attack. Choking for breath, my heart beating like a bomb about to go off, sweating through my sheets. When I finally woke up, I could barely move. It was like I was seeing everything through a filter of fog that dulled all the daylight and turned every color to gray. I felt so alone, so isolated, so worthless.

I silently willed myself to stand. *Just take out the fucking garbage*, I thought. *Just do that much, that's all. And then you can go back to bed.*

I grabbed our overflowing bag of trash, stumbled down our steps, and shuffled over to the dumpster. Suddenly I stopped. I looked around. I had never noticed it before, but the back alley of our little apartment building was bigger than you might think.

There was space for the dumpster, which fucking reeked, but still . . . it could be moved. There was room for six parking spots, half-tucked away under three overhanging units. I mean, cars used the spots all the time—this was LA—but I could do something about that. There were a few square feet of cracked asphalt dotted with cigarette butts and trash and some shards of glass. Someone could clean that up. Ideally not me. But someone. And our neighborhood was pretty quiet. We lived in North Hollywood— emphasis on the *North*. It wasn't glamorous, it was just concrete-covered, strip-mall-infested suburban sprawl.

In other words, it was perfect.

We could do a show here, I thought. *Or I could start selling a* lot *of drugs. Just not the weed—that's for me.*

And I knew exactly the ride-or-die, human labrador retriever I needed by my side. I pulled out my phone, pressed a button, and Paul picked up immediately.

"Bro," I said, "I am stressed out, I am cut off, and I need an outlet to be creative." He was the first person I told about how low I'd been feeling. Just opening up was enough to bring tears to my eyes. "We gotta put on a show."

"I'm at your service," he responded. Okay, a golden retriever—or maybe a creepy butler.

Lowkey Outside came to life. And I was reborn.

These were tougher negotiations than I'd ever experienced with any agent, producer, or club owner. None of those pros had anything on the crazy bitch who lived down the hall in my apartment.

"It's easy money," I told her. "You get fifty bucks for not complaining to management, and another hundred for letting us use your parking spot for the day."

She didn't even hesitate. "Make it two hundred."

Fuck. This was all me and Paul's own money. Yeah, we'd be selling tickets, but we'd be lucky to break even, at best.

"Come on," I pleaded. "We're just trying to do something fun here, all right? We aren't even gonna be making any money on this."

"Not my problem," she said with a shrug. "Two hundred."

This lady was elderly with stringy brown hair and thick librarian-style glasses, and she lived with her asshole brother, so I wanted to have empathy for her, but she was so obnoxious it was hard to care. She was the type of neighbor who would call the cops if you slurped your soup too loud, which meant she both sucked—*and* we had to be extra careful not to piss her off on the quickly approaching day of our very first show.

"Fine," I said with a sigh. "Two hundred."

I handed her a wad of bills and she slammed the door in my face. The bitch had just managed to get double what all the cool neighbors got for their spots. That's the American way, I guess.

As excited as Paul and I were to put on an actual live, flesh-and-blood comedy show for the first time in what felt like forever, we had dramatically underestimated how much work it would take to get ready for the show. It was set for a Saturday in July, which gave us about two weeks to do—what, wrangle a few chairs, get a mic and some speakers, maybe post a few flyers? How hard could it be?

Hard, apparently. Turns out that a dude who had spent most of the past few years couch surfing was not particularly prepared for complex logistics. Especially in a pandemic.

Getting comedians to perform was actually the easiest part. Sure, a few people we asked were still too worried about COVID to do anything live, no matter how safe we were. And I understood—comedians had families, they had kids, it simply wasn't worth the risk. But most stand-ups were just as eager to get in front of a live crowd as we were. Taylor Tomlinson, Iliza Shlesinger, and a bunch of our other buddies totally could not wait to do a set next to my dumpster.

Same goes for rounding up an audience. I figured we could fit about seventy people in my alley when it was all said and done. Grouping friends together was a little tricky because of safety requirements, but we posted that shit on Eventbrite and sold out overnight.

But the actual, you know, physical production of it all was a bit more challenging. What the hell were we gonna use as an actual stage? We couldn't just have the comics stand on their tiptoes on the asphalt. Could we?

What about liability? People sued over anything these days. I mean, Paul and I were so broke that there was no money to really sue us over, but that never stopped anyone.

Then there was the whole getting-sick thing. Putting on a show was all fine and good, but what if someone, like, died? That would put a real damper on things.

Paul and I had to scramble. And fast.

For the "stage," we rented a U-Haul. Comics could stand in the back, and at least they'd be elevated over the crowd.

For liability, we hired a high-powered attorney and made sure to get a city health permit so everything was completely legal. Which is all a total lie, of course. Really what we did was print out some generic form on the internet that said something like, "Hey, if I die or lose a limb, I won't sue anyone, pinky swear," for everyone in the audience to sign. Foolproof!

For actual health stuff, we really did take it seriously. More or less. We got one of our buddies to take people's temperatures as they walked in. What did doctors consider a fever again? Something like 103 degrees, right? Got it, cool. To make sure each seat was spaced six feet apart, we used the very scientific measurement of my right foot, which is precisely twelve inches long, give or take eleven inches or so—whatever, never really been good at "measuring stuff." Luckily, girls never know what eight inches actually looks like. I paced out the distances, and Paul filled out the rows. And my best friend James was in charge of passing out waters during the show, because water is totally healthy, right?

Oh, and for all the chairs themselves, we used a place called "On-Time Party Rentals," which was, of course, not on time, and never would be.

The big day finally arrived. And the pains in my ass officially began.

We started first thing in the morning by moving the cars (that bitch still managed to bitch!) and rolling the foul, greasy-ass dumpster out into the street (why didn't I make Paul do this?) and then sweeping up the cigarette butts and glass shards (why didn't I make him do this, too? Or James? Wasn't that what a best friend was for?).

Sweat was pouring off us, and I suddenly realized just how hot it was supposed to get that day—106 degrees on the pavement. We'd planned on holding the show during the middle of the afternoon so we could avoid renting a lighting rig, but we hadn't planned on a fucking heat wave, too. Paul frantically called up some friend of a friend who had done lighting on a couple indies and he agreed to rent us a fifteen-foot blacked-out screen that would provide shade to maybe half of our audience. It would only cost us five hundred dollars—which was about a hundred dollars more than the lighting rig would've cost. Huge win!

The comics started arriving, the audience started piling in, waivers were signed, temperatures were taken, masks were handed out, and I was greeting people and smiling under my mask and carefully fist-bumping. My blood was pumping, and I felt alive for the first time in months—and I had *just enough time* to take a shower before the show.

I was busy washing my hair—which you are now picturing, and you're welcome—when suddenly—

BAM! BAM! BAM!

Paul literally broke open my door with his shoulder.

"Dude," I said, "we're friends, and I really like you, but—"

"Cops are here!" he shouted. "It's a raid!"

FUCK.

That fucking bitch—after we gave her an extra hundred bucks and everything! She *still* ratted our asses out!

Sopping wet, soap in my hair, I threw on a towel and nothing else—hey, if we're gonna go down in flames, might as well give the crowd a good show—and scrambled down the stairs and outside. A cop was standing there, young and white, his hands on his belt, a frown on his face, all by the book like Officer Exley before he learns to play ball in *LA Confidential*.

"Um," I squeaked—I mean roared. "Can I help you?"

"What's going on back here?" he said.

"Uh . . . comedy show?" I croaked.

Seriously, what was I gonna say—Socially Distanced Neighborhood Watch?

We were done. It was over. I knew it. All the work we'd put in, all the money we'd spent, it was all gonna be for nothing. Worst of all, I was gonna be back to where I started—waking up in the middle of the afternoon every day, smoking weed, playing video games, doing nothing, feeling nothing, having nothing to live for. Shit.

Without saying a word, the young cop and his partner walked upstairs to one of the units. Paul and I looked at each other, shrugged. What was going on?

They walked inside the apartment and we could hear their walkies crackling. A few agonizing minutes passed. Finally, they walked downstairs, looked us up and down, strode over to their patrol cars, and just . . . left.

Wait a second—they left? Was this some kind of test? Were they about to call in SWAT? Were they just like, "Wow, this neighbor really *is* a bitch"? What the hell? Turned out it was just a domestic dispute, someone else's problem. Phew!

"Fuck it," I told Paul. "We got a show to put on."

Lowkey Outside ran for over a year, adding up to dozens of shows.

Were we flawless? Hell no! Sometimes a mic would go dead. Sometimes a comic would flake. Sometimes it would rain—in which case, Paul and I would "buy" a dozen beach tents from Home Depot and take them back soaked the next day for a full refund. Hey, the company slogan is "Doers Get More Done," right? We were more than happy to do on Home Depot's dime, thanks to their amazing return policy.

When helicopters buzzed overhead, we turned up the speakers. When it got freezing cold, we rented propane heaters. And when the back alley of my apartment building got too cramped, we expanded—in a big way.

We moved from there to a long driveway in the neighboring town of Eagle Rock to some very large parking lots in the Valley. We never posted the address online, because after that first encounter with the cops, I always wanted to play it safe. Plus, it gave the whole operation an air of mystery, of fighting the establishment. We went from crowds of seventy people to as many as four hundred. And we landed names as big as Jeff Ross, Tom Segura, and Bill Burr, paying them two hundred dollars for a set—just a *tiny bit* below their usual booking fee. Word of mouth spread, and comics just wanted to play our gig. Shoutout to Taylor T., though, who was always one of the biggest *Lowkey Outside* boosters.

Our show became something of a local comedy institution during the pandemic. We started using one of our friend's pickup trucks as a stage, and another friend took a photo of me and Paul standing in the back of it with our mics and turned it into our official logo. Jimmy Fallon's *Tonight Show* let one of our buddies, Jesus Trejo, shoot one of his sets live at *Lowkey Outside* so they could air it on NBC. Paul and I even got our very first article in *Deadline Hollywood*, one of the industry's top publications. It was like all these entertainment insiders suddenly decided, "Hey, maybe these two dudes in the back of a truck are really onto something."

Eventually the glow faded, of course. Isn't that how it always is? Other people started putting on their own guerilla comedy events. The mainstream clubs and big-time venues started welcoming audiences back inside. Eventually we stopped selling out every night, and gradually our crowds got smaller and smaller. The world was opening back up. Life was moving on.

But for me, what Paul and I had accomplished always felt like more than a show. It felt like more than an industry success story. More than a phenomenon, if you want to call it that. It felt personal. It felt like my friends, my community, and my love of stand-up had come together to help me find my way back from the brink.

It felt like I was ready to take on the world.

12

THE LAZY HERO

Doesn't eat ass!" has never exactly been a dealbreaker for me.

I mean, look—I like to fuck as much as the next dude. Maybe a little more, maybe a little less. Whatever, I'm not exactly out there taking anonymous polls (no pun intended). But other than my thing for women who are a little, shall we say, more mature in age, I'm basically a meat-and-potatoes guy when it comes to sex.

From missionary, to her on her stomach, her leg pulled up to the side where she's kinda on her stomach and her side at once—to a little love slap and an occasional *HAWK TUAH* in a fit of passion. If you're into it, choking is great—but from me to you. Don't collapse my airway while I cum from embarrassment. I'm a simple man, so when it comes to butt stuff, I'd say I'm a "don't ask, don't tell" kind of guy. As in, don't ask to go near mine, and don't tell me what's come out of yours. Truce.

Until one night when I was up onstage, doing one of my most tried-and-true bits about red flags in relationships. I was going through my list of things that were absolute nonstarters for me in any woman—normal, universal stuff, like any interest in satanism, for example—when a lady in the crowd suddenly, for some reason, decided to tell her own.

"What about eating ass!" the anonymous voice shouted. "*What if they won't eat ass?!*"

I'll be honest—I definitely didn't ask. But for the very first time I was all ears.

On the one hand, I'm not gonna pretend it was the most clever thing for a person to shout. As a performer, you learn pretty quick that the bluntest lines in comedy can often be the dullest. If you open with a gag that's blatantly crazy, it's hard to go anywhere but down after that. Plus, the audience can sense when someone is trying too hard to get a laugh—whether that someone is up onstage or sitting a couple rows down. It feels inauthentic, like you're just trying to get attention, and it can prompt an eyeroll faster than a smile.

On the other hand, it opened up a whole world of new opportunities for me. Again, not in bed—but in my act. I'd been talking about my own red flags for ages at this point. If anything, I was getting a little tired of the routine. But what about *my fans'* red flags? I'm not gonna pretend to be some kind of overbearing feminist or something, but I had a mom, I had a sister, I had a bunch of girls who were good friends, and I knew enough to know that women wanted to be heard, to be listened to—not just talked at.

What if I started opening up the act to them? Sure, some of it might eat shit—perhaps too literally—but some of it could be comedy gold. Why the hell not? I was only giving one side of the red flag, I needed perspective!

"Not tonight, y'all," I said to the crowd. "But I'll bring a few breath mints or a stick of gum next time, and maybe I'll make up for it."

In the back of my mind, I'd already bought a big-ass pack of Big League Chew.

By the time I got to the Copper Blues club just north of Phoenix in the summer of 2022, I was fucking exhausted.

Life on the road might sound kind of glamorous, and I get it. For a guy like me, any chance to perform my comedy wasn't just a blessing, it was a miracle. How many aspiring comics or actors had I met in LA, fresh off the bus from Nebraska, who ended up going home on the exact same bus a couple years later? Or even worse, they decided to move to Florida? This industry is *hard*. You have to be not just talented, not just tough, you need to be lucky as hell. I grabbed any opportunity to get onstage and make people laugh, no matter where that stage happened to be.

If someone gave me a shot to tell jokes in front of a "crowd" of seventeen people on a Thursday night in an Indian casino in Oklahoma—bro, I was there. No questions asked.

But I ain't gonna lie—the lifestyle can be brutal on the body and mind. Back then, I was doing anything I could to save a dime, so there were no breaks, no going home to recharge, no nothing. It could be my first night in New York, my second night in Philly, then Boston the next night, followed by Virginia the night after that. And I couldn't afford to fly, so usually I was driving myself from one place to the next in a hatchback economy rental. The few times I actually could fly, it was the cheapest of the cheap, on Spirit or Southwest, trying to fold my six-foot frame into this tiny seat at a ninety-degree angle. There's nothing to lean on, you're hunched over your tray, and your forehead is leaving grease smears on the window. Sleep? Never happens. Glamour? On Spirit? Are you crazy?

And when you do finally get to that city or town, you're not going out and seeing the sights. There's no fine dining or games at Madison Square Garden, or even crap tables at the Indian casinos. You get to your venue, you do your work, you cash in your free drink ticket at the overpriced bar, then you head to your mid-tier hotel. I can find my way from the lobby to the shower of a Courtyard Marriot with my eyes closed. I can smell a La Quinta a whole county over. I will for the rest of my life think a normal bar of soap is massive. If you're lucky—I mean really lucky—maybe you got a couple other of your broke comic buddies with you, so you can cry together about how miserable your life is, then admit that there's nothing else you'd rather do.

In fact, you're loving every fucking second. Who the hell knows why.

That's pretty much where my head was at by the time I got to Arizona. I was actually headlining the show that night—not because I was a big deal, but because every now and then a club would do me a favor and be like, "Here's our worst weekend of the year. You headline, we'll send out a random email blast to all the bots on our list, offering them free tickets, then if any of them actually show up, hopefully we'll get them drunk enough to make back our money. You're welcome."

But all things considered, Copper Blues was a pretty sweet little venue. It wasn't exactly Arizona's finest, but it could hold a couple hundred people, there was a nice restaurant attached and all my food was comped, and the club was even gonna let a couple of my buddies open for me.

Plus, I had something different I wanted to try.

By this point, I'd fallen out of love with social media *hard*. I'd call it a love-hate relationship except, yeah—it was almost all hate. I mean, I was on all the usuals—Instagram, Facebook, Twitter, whatever—because I pretty much had no choice. As a struggling comic, I needed to reach potential fans wherever and however I could find them. Sure, maybe all my postings only got me an extra twenty people to that Indian casino show in Oklahoma, but when you're talking about a total audience of forty, you'd sell any extra ticket you could.

Plus, I really had been able to reach a relatively small but amazingly engaged core of people who really were into me and my comedy—an actual *community*—and I appreciate those early adopters to this day. In 2021, right in the middle of the pandemic, while Paul Elia and I were putting on *Lowkey Outside*, I decided to take shit to a whole new level by shooting my very first hour-long special, in the same spirit as Lowkey. I wasn't trying to get famous—not that a little fame wouldn't have been nice—I just wanted to create something, you know? Put something out in the universe and see what happened.

There was just one issue—how to pay for the thing. Yeah, not a minor issue. But I turned to my community through crowdfunding, and not only did they help me meet my goal of fifteen thousand, they also got me an extra ten thousand dollars on top of that. Which is why when you watch my special it doesn't look like some bootstrapped production made for YouTube. It looks about as good as anything you'd find on Netflix. Well, maybe Tubi. I called it *Only Fans* because it really was by and for my fans—though a few people probably clicked on it with their lube at the ready. But even that was intentional—to drive traffic.

So I fucking love the real ones who've found me on social media. And a lot of y'all are straight-up, ride-or-die real ones, and I love you for it.

But let's be straight—some of y'all try my patience. And I'm not even talking about crazy shit, like harassment or stalking or whatever. That nonsense is irritating, but you can filter it out if you have to. I'm talking about the little things that *drive you* crazy.

How many times have I posted a flyer that says, "Guess what—I'm coming to Denver next week!" And then I get twenty comments under that same post that all go, "But bro, when you coming to Denver??" Or I do a special post announcing a new city I just added to a world tour, then—I shit you not—I'll get all these people saying, "Dude, how can it be a world tour?? It's only *one city!!* "

Okay, you got me, guys. I was trying to pass off a world tour when it was really just a single night in Tallahassee. I really thought I could pull one over on y'all, but you're just too sharp for me.

But as annoying as it is to figure out twenty new things to post a day to feed the content beast, you gotta do social media. Even if it's a toxic, full-time job *on top of* your real full-time job—you gotta do it. Even if there's so much negativity, it drowns out any and all positive messages—you gotta do it. Which is why when TikTok came out, I took a deep breath and said, "You gotta do it."

And if I was gonna do it, I was gonna do it right.

I went out and spent a few hundred hard-earned dollars that I didn't have to spare on a camera that wouldn't break, and I spent an afternoon with my buddy Elton, who showed me the basics of video editing on Premiere Pro—creating projects, resizing sequences, zooming and tracking movements on the screen—and also let me record his lesson on my phone. Partly because he's a great friend, and partly because he didn't want to have to keep answering all my dumb-ass questions over and over again.

I started recording and posting clips from my live shows on TikTok and all the other platforms, and I had just started doing my new interactive Red Flag routine. And guess what? Just like I'd expected, most of it did eat shit. In fact, so far it *all* had—garnering me just a few thousand views here and there, which in modern social media amounted to nothing.

It wasn't exactly fun. My passion was performing onstage. I hadn't broken into comedy to be some kind of social media influencer. My camera started to feel like that expensive gym membership you can't get out of. You fucking hate the place, you'd rather be sitting at home smoking weed, but they just charged you $250 for the month of June, so I guess it's time to do a goddamn squat.

But I still held out a tiny bit of hope. Maybe, just maybe, by opening up this world of inter-crowd communication in this Red Flag bit, I'd finally strike gold. Maybe I would even get it on film.

Maybe it would happen tonight in Arizona.

I was setting my camera up near a table in the back when suddenly I heard the announcer.

"Everybody help me welcome Matt Rife . . ."

Fuck! I hit record, hoped the camera was in focus, and sprinted up to the stage to a smattering of applause. I quickly scanned the crowd. Maybe seventy people? Like a third full? They were scattered in these awkward little clumps throughout the mostly empty room. This was the audience you got from a tiny social media following and a generic email blast from the club, offering free tickets to anyone with a pulse.

Whatever. A perfect chance to try some new material.

"All right," I said right after I finished my typical Red Flag bit.

"How 'bout y'all? What are some of the biggest red flags for women about guys? Come on, don't be shy."

Not that they needed much encouragement. I'd found out pretty quick that people *wanted* to share. They loved it, almost needed it. Maybe it had something to do with the question—who doesn't love to bitch about an ex? Maybe it had something to do with the crowd, which was usually mostly women—I have no idea why, but it definitely is *not* because I look like every MILF's poolboy fantasy. Or maybe it's just my natural charm.

"Flip-flops!" someone shouted.

"Mama's boy!" someone yelled.

"Doesn't eat ass!" someone screamed.

Honestly, it's amazing how much that one comes up. What the hell is wrong with y'all? Go to church.

And maybe, when I'd first started engaging with my audience, I would've heard one of those options and taken a bite—sorry, just way too easy—but not anymore. A lot of comics are taught that the best way to do crowd work is to *not* be spontaneous. Have a few well-honed zingers ready, then go fishing in the crowd until you find the setup you need. *Oh, he said he's a dentist! Now I can use my killer root canal joke!* (Note to all aspiring comics: There is no such thing as a killer root canal joke. We get it, he gave her a filling.)

But what I'd been learning was that the best material didn't come from practiced one-liners. I'd honed my improv skills in the wild environment of *Wild 'N Out*, so I knew that spontaneity wasn't the enemy—it was the key. Creativity comes from specificity, and specificity comes from real conversation. Almost like a first date. You've gotta be comfortable with pretty much anyone—Black, white, disabled, whoever. And you've gotta be vulnerable. No one wants to talk to an arrogant prick whose only goal is to flex. For someone to open up, they need to feel like they're in control. It's up to you to create that energy, to naturally guide the back-and-forth, to never feel like you're trying too hard.

It's something I learned doing comedy in front of so many Black audiences in my career—they could smell the fear in a white boy like me, so I could never fake it. I had to be myself and trust that everything would work out.

But for everything to work out, I needed a starting point, an opener . . .

"He doesn't do anything!"

And now I have it.

The voice comes from somewhere out to my left. I shade my eyes with my hand so I can see farther back in the club, and I spot her—a woman in her thirties sitting at a table with a couple other people. What the fuck does she mean by "He doesn't do anything"?

I have no idea, and that's the beauty of it. These four words just opened up a whole universe of absurdity for me to explore.

"He didn't do anything wrong?" I ask incredulously. "Or in life?"

"In life," she says.

My mind races. It's impossible to do *nothing* in life. Impossible! Time to dive in.

"He didn't have a job the entire time you guys were together?" I say. No judgment here—not yet—just curiosity. Just an invitation to open up.

"He did," she responds.

Um, okay, I think. And then she says it.

"He works in the ER!"

Wait, *what?* Instantly an image takes shape in my mind in 4K res.

An exhausted man in scrubs returns home from a rough night at the hospital. Coffee and adrenaline still in his veins, he's too tired to sleep, so he just zones out in the quiet of the evening. That bus that jackknifed on the interstate? You saw it on the news—what they could show, at least.

We were able to save seven lives, he thinks, but we lost one. And it's the ones you lose that you count. Not the ones you save. All your train-ing, all your effort—does it even matter? Does anything really matter?

He closes his eyes, exhales, and hears his girlfriend behind him.

"Wow . . . so you're just not gonna come to Amber's karaoke birth-day party tonight, huh?"

This is a live wire and we are on the record, people!

"Oh, I'm sorry," I say without missing a beat. "You broke up with a *hero*."

The crowd is starting to lose their shit. I've got her.

"So how did he not do anything if he worked in the ER?" I say. "Was he the janitor?"

"Well, aside from work," she replies, "he didn't do anything."

"Aside from work he didn't do anything," I repeat after her, legitimately mystified. Basically, this lady is saying that her ex was a hero . . . but a *lazy* hero. Could this be it? The gold I'd been hoping to find for so long? "He was *saving lives!*" I shout. "You don't think when Superman gets done, he needs to chill?"

Bam! I get the explosion of laughter I was hoping for. I love it, feed off it. I decide to turn the screw. "What do *you* do?"

"*Yeah!*" someone shouts in the audience. They're cheering me on. They want vindication! They want justice for this unappreciated, hard-working man! They want—

"I work for American Airlines!" she proudly proclaims.

Perfection.

How the fuck do you work for American Airlines and have United standards? This lady puts your tray table up for a living, while her do-nothing boyfriend is busy sewing bullet wounds at three a.m. Ladies and gentlemen, we have a hypocrite!

Now the floodgates are open.

"Fuck you!" I shout, literally flipping her off. "*Where are my bags???*"

It's a huge risk on my part, because I don't want to be perceived as the bad guy in the bit, but guess what? My instincts are right on. She tells me she literally works in the baggage department.

Hell, at least a stewardess hands out peanuts to an ungrateful public. They even have to duct-tape motherfuckers to their seats every now and then! That's at least *something*. But no. She's the one who stonewalls you with a "Sir!" or a "Ma'am!" and puts you on a ten-minute hold. When you're in Connecticut and your luggage is in Detroit, folks, this is who you have to thank. What we have here is as close to a perfect modern villain as we're ever going to get. And her boyfriend is a contemporary saint saving lives every day.

Ladies, if you need someone who can give you more time and attention, don't date a guy who works at a hospital. Date a homeless dude. Sure, maybe Tent City Tony never pays for anything and always wants to stay over, but he's always down for an adventure, he loves the outdoors, and he has a "rescue" dog—exactly what you said you wanted on your Hinge profile. So open your heart, Stacey.

Or if you do wanna go for a doctor, maybe, I don't know . . . relax? Let the man breathe. Manage your expectations. Or hope that the next time he's sewing on an arm, the patient decides to stage an intervention for you: "Doc, please, leave it—I have another arm. Why are you *here* when there's a new flea market your girl wants to hit up before ten a.m.?"

I finished my set at Copper Blues to a roar of laughter and applause. "This," I said, "is why there's two sides to every story!"

Seventy people seemed happy with how the show went—actually, seventy-one. I was pretty happy, too. The Red Flags interactions were working better and better every time I went up onstage. It felt like I was hitting a vein with my audience. I checked my camera, made sure it had recorded, and broke down my tripod. Shook a few hands, hugged my comedian friends who'd performed earlier that night, and went back to my hotel room.

I had captured my whole show on my fancy camera. But once I started editing the footage—even chronic insomnia can be productive sometimes—the "Lazy Hero" bit didn't seem quite as exceptional as it had felt in real time. Yeah, the lady in the crowd had said some ridiculous things, and our conversation was authentic, the flow felt natural. But I'm a perfectionist. I regarded it like a chef tasting a sauce he was still trying to get right. It wasn't bad, but it wasn't exactly there yet. It was nothing more than a solid night's work. I closed my laptop and got into bed.

I decided to not even post the video.

The next day, I woke up, had a quick breakfast, hit the airport, and crammed my body into yet another economy seat. No one recognized me, and there was no parade when I landed back in LA. I got an alert from my bank that the club had paid me. When I factored in travel and what I'd paid my openers, I probably cleared a couple hundred bucks on the gig.

If you had told me as I Uber Pooled back to my apartment that my entire life was about to change, I would have said you were crazy. But it was.

13

WTF

A few weeks later, me and my boy Paul Elia arrived at one of comedy's biggest, most important parties of the year—I mean, some of the hottest comics and most influential producers were at this thing. And all I could think about was how loud to get when I told the organizers to go fuck themselves.

Yeah, in case you haven't noticed, I got a big-ass chip on my shoulder, dude. And if you're one of the many, many people who've added to that chip? You can get ready to hear about it from me. I am not a "turn-the-other-cheek" kind of guy. I'm a big fan of grudges. They keep me warm at night when I'm having a hard time sleeping, like a nice thin blanket covered in broken glass and razor blades. If you fuck me over, I will never, ever let it go.

The guys in charge of the Just For Laughs Festival in Montreal were about to find that out. It was July of 2022, just a month after my "Lazy Hero" set at Copper Blues, and I still hadn't posted the video of the bit online. In fact, it couldn't have been farther from my mind. Right now, I was focused on payback for the boys of JFL.

For decades, Just For Laughs had been the premiere stand-up festival pretty much in the whole world. Its New Faces Show especially is famous for breaking out young new comics. Everyone from Kevin Hart to Amy Schumer to Dave Chappelle had popped off breakout sets there, going from reasonably successful to being household names. The entire city of Montreal came alive for the festival. There was the Just For Laughs main stage, there were smaller shows at every bar and club in town, there was pure, non-stop stand-up at all hours of the day and night. It was one massive orgy of laughter.

And for almost as long, these dudes had wanted nothing to do with me. I'd auditioned four or five times for the New Faces Show—the show was considered such a big deal that just auditioning was nerve-racking as hell. And even though I'd earned a standing ovation at one audition in particular, I'd been rejected by Just For Laughs over and over with no explanation. Which was annoying, but it was the business. Sometimes, for whatever reason, shit just didn't break your way. Whatever. I got it.

But then in 2022, the Just For Laughs organizers decided they wanted to feature the guerilla comedy show that Paul and I had started during the pandemic in LA. They wanted to bring *Lowkey*

Outside to Montreal. There was just one problem. They didn't want to bring me.

Now shit was getting personal.

Weeks before the festival, the Just For Laughs people seriously got in touch with Paul and—no joke—were like, *Hey, we really love this cool show that you and Matt Rife literally founded together, right next to the dumpster behind Matt Rife's apartment. How about you put it on for us in Canada . . . without Matt Rife?*

They wanted to split up Hall & Oates. Tear apart Cheech & Chong. Drive a wedge between chocolate and peanut butter. And worst of all—*I* was Oates! *I* was Chong! *I* was peanut butter! I was the half no one really wanted, all rolled into one. And it was just as messy as it sounds. Probably would've tasted like shit, too.

Yet again, Just For Laughs gave no explanation, no rationale, no nothing except "Yeahhh, we don't want this guy." I love Paul like a brother, so I was like, "Look, dude, this is a great opportunity for you and your career. If they won't let me join, you should just do it."

Paul was like, "Yeah, fuck them. You're coming."

He told the organizers that if I couldn't do it, he wouldn't do it either. It was both of us or nothing at all. And they caved—kind of.

The bookers said I could come, but I still wouldn't be allowed to host it. Paul and a Canadian comic named Dave Merheje— actually a pretty cool, funny guy—would still do that. But they'd let me do my own eight-minute set during the show. Awesome, right? Like, thank you for giving me permission to appear in the event I created.

167

Just For Laughs also very generously agreed to give me and Paul a grand total of five hundred dollars to cover all our expenses. And if you didn't catch the sarcasm there, you're probably one of the geniuses who really thought I was trying to hit on Zendaya. That was $250 a person for round-trip tickets—on Spirit, of course—plus a crummy, overpriced Airbnb in Montreal's busiest, most booked weekend of the year. Meaning that sleeping on the couch would continue to be the single biggest theme of my career.

I felt completely humiliated. But I needed this. My career needed this. There was nothing I could do but suck it up and accept their bullshit terms.

Now here I was for the big opening-night welcome bash. And I was doing my best to put on a good face—I mean, honestly, I really do have a very good face—because I knew I needed to make the most of my time here. I mean, this entire festival was full of execs and talent scouts who could change my life if they wanted.

But I was also pissed.

The whole city of Montreal just seemed phony as hell. Everything about it was trying so hard to scream "We're so cultured! We're so French and European! Forget about the fact that we're like an hour away from Bumblefuck, New York, and have another skinny fucking bagel!" And it's like—sorry, dude. Poutine? French fries would've made sense, but putting gravy on them is pretty on-brand American. You're just as trash as the rest of us. You're just trash with a couple big buildings and an annoying accent.

This party wasn't much better. I could see the organizers greeting everyone. Smiles painted on their faces, shaking hands, giving out hugs, laughing like crazy at every joke, no matter how stale. And all I could think was—*What are these fuckers gonna do when they see me? Are they gonna act like they haven't spent the last few years doing everything they could to screw me over? Are they just gonna pretend we're the best of friends? Or will they at least have the balls to say something—obviously not an apology, they'd never do that. But any kind of admission whatsoever? Even a "Hey, we're glad we made this work"?*

Like, throw me a bone, motherfuckers! Then I'll decide if I should break it in half.

The bookers walked over, all smiles and back-slapping, and immediately I knew. Of course I did. This was always how it was gonna be.

"Paul! Matt!" they gushed. "We are *so happy* to see you!"

Okay, fine. If that was how they wanted it.

"Oh really?" I said with a smirk. "Because I wasn't invited. In fact, I was kinda surprised y'all let me in tonight. I figured security would stop me at the door."

Paul laughed nervously and pulled me away. Just as I was getting warmed up.

Now, I'd like to tell you that what I said made some kind of impact with these people. That they looked shocked by my breach of protocol, or at least mildly embarrassed. Hell, I would've been happy with a slightly crinkled brow. But nope. They didn't register a word I said. Probably weren't even listening. Just bobbed their heads and grinned and moved right on to their next phony conversation without missing a beat.

It was day two in Montreal, just a couple hours before we were scheduled to go up for Lowkey, and I was having an early dinner at a random chain restaurant with my two closest confidants in the world: Paul, the ride-or-die who almost literally would've died before letting Just For Laughs kick me off our show, and Christina Shams, my current manager. My very first manager, Gary Abdo, was still a good friend of mine—still is—but I had started working with Christina to take my career to the next level. So far, with less than spectacular results.

And I was feeling like shit. I mean, yeah, giving the festival organizers some attitude right to their face had been a nice little buzz. But now I was thinking about later tonight, when I'd have to perform a solo set on my very own show because I wasn't allowed to host it. I was thinking about all the times casting agents would tell me "you're so talented" followed by "but you're not what we're looking for." I was thinking about the last ten years and how far I'd come—without going very far at all.

Hell, even my wins were barely moving the needle. My self-produced, crowdfunded special, *Only Fans*, had gotten over a million views on YouTube, better than I'd ever expected in my wildest dreams. But I was still flying Spirit and sharing crummy Airbnbs on a budget of $250. And we had fought for the privilege!

I needed a change. A big fucking change.

"You know what I should do?" I said. "I should just join the military."

"Bro," Paul said, shooting me a skeptical look. "The military? For real?"

"Dude," I said, "I've got a whole tradition of service in my family. It's nothing to scoff at."

And it was true. Grandpa Steve wasn't the only one who'd been in the navy. My uncle and my great-grandpa had both been in the navy, too. When I was a little kid, I'd had dreams of being a fighter pilot, but I have shit vision, so that was out. Maybe the army? After years of having no real schedule or career stability, there was something appealing about a lifestyle that was nothing but structure and taking orders.

Wake up and go to bed at the same time every day. Work out a few times. Eat your three squares. What did they feed you in the military anyway? Meat? Potatoes? Slop? Whatever, I wasn't picky. I was sure the military slop was really delicious slop. And I bet my cot would be a lot more comfortable than a sofa. A little stiff, yeah, but decent support for my back . . .

"Matt!" Christina said, snapping me out of it. "Earth to Matt! I hate to break it to you, but you are not joining the military, okay?"

"Why not?"

"Because! Comedy is in your blood! You've been through too much to quit now. You have too much to offer to give up. And I won't let you."

I smiled. If you've actually been paying attention—and of course you totally have—you remember Christina Shams from when I first moved to LA and my comedian buddy Erik Griffin was begging her to give me stage time at the Laugh Factory. Tall, Persian, oddly genuine, she had left the club years ago to be an agent. Very long story, she became my agent on a whim, and when I decided to leave that agency, I begged her to start working as my manager. I loved her because she was the one person I'd ever worked with who never told me no.

Every other agent I'd met had a ready-made excuse for why basically everything I suggested was doomed to fail. *You want to leave* Wild 'N Out? *Who cares if they're pigeonholing you, take the money. What? Shoot your own special? Who cares about your fans, that won't do anything. Wait, you want to pitch people a TV show about hot teenagers? Oh, none of the networks are looking for that, total waste of time.*

Then like a week later fucking *Riverdale* comes out. Great work, guys.

Don't get me wrong. Plenty of my ideas end up being shit. It's the nature of the business. The nature of creativity. But if my ideas don't work, at least I only have myself to blame. If I let someone talk me out of it, I'll always wonder "what if." Shams always trusted me, and that meant the world.

In this case, though, I was okay with Christina talking me out of it. Now that I thought about it, I'd heard funny people don't do well in the military. Drill sergeants aren't big fans of smart-asses talking out of turn. Pretty sure I saw a scene about that in *Full Metal Jacket.*

"What the hell should I do?" I said. "I gotta do something. Anything! And apparently, it can't be the army."

I started pushing around the bland fettuccine alfredo that was on my plate and absent-mindedly fiddling with my phone. I randomly popped open the clip of my "Lazy Hero" bit. It was about two and a half minutes long, and I'd never even posted it. I'd watched it a few times myself in the month since I shot and edited the thing, and each time it seemed less special.

Okay, so the lady thought her boyfriend was lazy. What was original about that? What was different? Who the fuck even cared anymore?

"Hey," Paul said, noticing my screen. "Just post it and eat."

"What's the point?" I said with a shrug. "It's not even funny, and no one will even see it."

So far, my experiments with the supposedly magical platform of TikTok had resulted in exactly jack shit. I'd post a clip and it would get fifty thousand views. Maybe a hundred thousand if I got lucky. Nothing but minor turds in the giant cesspool of social media, given that TikTok had well over a billion users by now.

Why was I even trying to matter online? The show had felt special in the moment, to me and the small crowd at Copper Blues. Wasn't that all that really mattered? Live comedy is irreplaceable, and nothing is as good as the real thing in the real moment.

"Bro," Paul said, who as a human golden retriever was starting to get vaguely annoyed at my shit attitude. "It's already edited! Just post it and forget about it. It definitely won't hurt."

My boy was always positive. Always.

I looked down at my phone and considered hitting post. I felt like a dude about to send a risky text. You know how it is, guys. That first dick pic can go terribly wrong—or wonderfully right. It's gonna be life-changing one way or another. If it goes right, you could be staring at a gorgeous, pixilated pic of two-dimensional tits from this girl in a matter of moments.

And if it goes wrong . . . well, I couldn't tell ya. And no, it's not because my dick is all that. It's because, bros—if there's even a hint of doubt in your mind that it will not go well, do *not* send that dick pic. Read the room, ya weirdos.

This time, though, I was gonna damn the torpedoes. So to speak. I hit post, muted my alerts, and put it out of my mind.

Erik Griffin, who's probably the closest thing I have to a comic mentor in this crazy business, always had what I thought was the strangest advice.

He'd say that if you wanted to put on your best show, you had to stop caring.

At first I took him super literally, to the point that his words of wisdom were borderline offensive. Like, *Dude, real people pay real money to go to these shows. This could be their one time all week—all month!—to forget about their problems and laugh for a while. And you want me to not care?*

But that night in Montreal, I learned that he meant something completely different. Erik wasn't saying that I shouldn't respect my audience and try to give them a great show. He was saying that to give them a great show, I needed to learn to let go. I needed to realize that I'd have good shows, and I'd have bad shows, and that was okay. Life would go on. The more I stopped worrying about giving people the perfect show, the better my chance of giving them the perfect show.

Erik, let me tell you, man—that was some real Yoda shit. And you were right. Because that's exactly what happened at the Lowkey Comedy Show at Just For Laughs.

I went up there with nothing to lose and nothing to prove. I forgot about my career, I forgot about all the failures, I forgot about all the slights, I forgot about the comedic equivalent of a dick pic I'd just posted to TikTok. And I had fun. I did my set by myself, and then Paul came up afterwards and it was like we were back in LA hosting together. The same chemistry, the same magic, the same merciless roasting of each other.

And we absolutely killed.

The crowd came to life, they were totally with us every step of the way, and we all fed off each other's energy. It really, truly was some real Yoda shit. All of a sudden, getting almost no money to fly myself on Spirit Air seemed like a small, insignificant detail. There would always be time to take on the big issues. Those demons would be sitting on the edge of my Airbnb couch the next morning.

I went to sleep that night with all my cynicism shaken off, at least temporarily. I was grateful that Paul stuck by me when Just For Laughs tried to break us up. Grateful that Christina had talked me out of getting my ass kicked by Sergeant Slaughter in the army. Grateful that, for the very first time in my life, I had managed to let go and just be.

Was it a coincidence that when I woke up the next morning everything in my life had suddenly changed? I have no fucking clue.

I'm definitely not into any kind of organized religion. I don't even know if I'd call myself "spiritual," that amazingly generic term that people use for everything from sticking pins in voodoo dolls to getting an ankh tattooed above their ass crack. And I think anyone who thanks God when they find a great parking spot or finally land a role on a TV show is kinda missing the point. Really? You went from being a heathen to a born-again Christian because you booked a three-episode arc on *NCIS*? Got it.

But I've seen some weird shit in my few years on this earth. Shit that honestly can't be explained by anything but the supernatural. I've seen furniture move without a hand on it. I've seen electronic devices start going crazy when they have no business even being turned on. And yes, I've smoked copious amounts of very potent, high-quality weed—but what could that possibly have to do with anything?

I know this all sounds crazy, but I think there might be a force out there. Some kind of energy in the universe that balances things out. Something that can only step in when it feels like you're out of options, when you've completely run out of ideas for how your life is *supposed* to go. Something that pulled me back from the edge every time I was about to give up on my dream.

That's the only explanation I really have for what happened the day after I posted my month-old "Lazy Hero" clip. Because when I checked my phone at the Airbnb in Montreal that morning, the clip was already at ten million views. And climbing.

I put my glasses on and blinked my eyes.

What. The. Fuck.

I shook Paul awake and called up Christina, the two friends who had given me such amazing wisdom the day before.

What. The. Fuck.

I mean, it was a fun, sweet little video. I was being hard on myself when I'd decided it was no good, which is something I have a tendency to do. But still. For it to do *this??* I'd posted plenty of other clips, even other crowd work clips, and nothing had ever popped off like this. Not even close.

For some reason, at the exact moment when I'd finally learned to let go, to surrender myself to whatever the universe had in store for me, that video went lab-leak viral. Over the next twenty-four hours alone, it went from ten million to twenty million—twenty million!—and it only kept growing from there. The infamous Tik-Tok algorithm did the rest. The platform started pushing my other clips, and suddenly stale old videos that I thought were dead were getting millions of views, devoured by an audience that loved what it saw and wanted more.

As my audience grew and grew, Christina knew exactly what to do. She started contacting every booking agent she knew, whipping up interest in the actual, you know, real world. People started to talk, and word of mouth spread. Fast.

By the time I got back to Los Angeles from Montreal—still crammed into my cramped seat on Spirit Air—my life was already getting very, very different.

The plane's wheels hit the tarmac, I turned on my phone, and the thing started shaking like a slot machine that hit the jackpot. Suddenly every comedy club owner and promoter in the country—people who wouldn't have even taken my call days earlier—were calling me.

And they all said the same thing: *We want Matt.*

14

ASHES FROM A SEX TOY

I had an idea. And when I have an idea that means trouble.

"All right, Papaw," I said, dialing up my grandpa Steve on the phone. "I got a little something I want you to help me out on."

He hesitated. Probably because he knew me well enough to know that "help" could mean just about anything, good or bad.

"Okay, then," he said slowly, and I could hear him roll the chaw around in his mouth, which was both hilarious and disgusting. "What kinda help you need?"

"I'm gonna give you a call tomorrow night between eight and eight thirty, all right? And when I do, here's what I want you to say . . ."

Which is how my grandpa Steve ended up appearing in the opening of my 2021 self-produced special *Only Fans*. The camera slowly pushes deep inside my dressing room—get your mind out of the trash, that's a very technical cinematography term; right past my boy Paul Elia, sitting checking his phone—no idea why he's there, but he is; and catches me FaceTiming with Papaw, pitching him names for the special as a few choice T-shirts hang on the wall.

"Okay, what about 'Problemattic'?" I ask him.

"No," he says.

"Toy Boy."

"No," he sighs.

"Okay, what do you think I should call it?"

Then, with the kind of flawless timing and dead-pan delivery you just can't teach: "It doesn't matter what you call it. They're just there to see you naked."

Aaaand scene.

There's a reason my grandpa was always my biggest inspiration. It's not only because he let me spend every weekend with him while I was growing up in Ohio and trying to escape my stepdad. It's not only because he literally bought my way into the open mic at my very first comedy club and never gave up on me. It's because my man was funny as hell.

More than anyone in my life, I tried to involve my grandpa Steve in my life and career. Not just him, by the way. To make it in comedy, you really can't make it all on your own. I'd say "It takes a village," but that phrase has always made me want to puke, and I fucking hate politicians. So I'll say it takes an entire community, an ecosystem of support, where you all got each other's back—no matter what. That can be family, that can be friends, that can even be your most devoted fans.

Now that I was finally starting to find some success, I wanted to start paying people back. I wanted to bring my community of support along for the ride. Don't get me wrong—even once "Lazy Hero" popped off and started driving millions of new fans to my comedy on TikTok, it wasn't like I turned into some kind of superstar overnight. Yeah, I was getting a lot more gigs, and a lot of them were at clubs that had never even returned my calls before. But it wasn't like I went straight from practically paying my own way to Just For Laughs to selling out stadiums across the country. That was still gonna take a ton of work—and not a little luck. I don't know how it works for other comics, but for me there's never been a single moment of "Oh, I've made it." It's always been "Jesus, I hope this is real . . ."

At the same time, though, my momentum was undeniable. Slowly but surely, my life was changing. And that meant I could begin to change the lives of the people I cared about, too.

I started with my friends. For them, I got the most sumptuous, decadent gift that people in Hollywood dream of. Forget about Bentleys or bling or cribs in Beverly Hills. No, I gave these motherfuckers jobs.

For years I'd had to beg every comic from Finesse Mitchell to my mentor Erik Griffin to let me open for them when they hit the road, just so I could make a few bucks, and I always appreciated how they took care of their crew. Now it was my turn to do the same. I got my buddy Alex—the guy who will *not* shut up, no matter how much you tell him to shut up—to start opening for me, which he does to this day. We started out sharing a room—but not a bed, I swear—and then I could finally afford to get him a room of his own, so at least I could get a break from his bullshit sometimes. I was able to hire another friend to be my videographer, another to be my photographer.

And yeah, shit could get awkward. Like when I'd have to be like, "I know all y'all want to do is smoke weed all day, because all *I* want to do is smoke weed all day—but we gotta fucking work!" But who am I kidding? I loved having my boys around. I went from sitting in random green rooms making awkward small talk with weird-ass local comics—because *all* comics are weird, and most of us smell like ass—to basically living my life like it was a permanent high school sleepover. Eating as much junk food as we wanted, playing video games, no bedtime, no rules. And of course, right after I yelled at people for smoking too much weed, I inevitably followed that up with: "Okay, fine, just another hour."

Usually followed immediately in my head by "WHY THE FUCK IS EVERYONE LAUGHING? THE ENTIRE TOUR IS FALLING APART!" Because, yeah, bad weed can do that to you sometimes.

Eventually, as I made some real money for the first time in my life, I was also able to help out my family. Sometimes in very big, very meaningful ways—just a little while ago, I was able to buy my mom her dream house. It was the least I could do for a woman who'd given me the space and support I needed to leave home and high school early to follow my dream in LA. I mean, think about it—this woman loved me and my sister like crazy.

She drove all the way down to Georgia just to watch me *audition* for *Wild 'N Out*. Her kids were her life, but she had the strength to let me go. Of course, it also didn't hurt that by this point she'd divorced my abusive stepdad. I would've been happy to give him a punch in the mouth. New house? Not so much.

Then there was my grandpa Steve. For that guy, I found the perfect way to start paying him back long before I became a star. It wasn't quite as big—actually, the model I found was supposed to be pretty damn tight—but it was very, very meaningful.

By this point, my papaw had been living by himself for fifteen years.

Fifteen years. Alone. Single. Without even going on so much as a date. It was just him, his plastic-covered furniture, his grievances against the world—and his hand. So my boy had carpal tunnel in joints he didn't even know existed. If he knew about internet porn, he would've been through three Tommy John surgeries.

A few years earlier he'd come out to LA to join me for a friends Christmas, and for the first time I could remember, he'd broken out of his shell. Cooking a huge meal for everyone, laughing, having fun, never smoking weed himself—but probably getting a decent contact high off the rest of us. I really thought the guy was gonna change.

Like, "What do you want to use for your profile pic, Papaw? The one of you in the black trucker hat? Or the one of you in . . . the other black trucker hat?"

Then COVID happened. And in case you were wondering, a global pandemic is exactly the worst thing for trying to convince a fucking hermit he needs to switch his life around. For literal years I'd been telling this dude he needed to get out more, and he finally had an excuse even I couldn't shut down: *Matt, have you looked out your window?* No one *is getting out more.* It was like a shut-in's paradise. They'd always told us that society wasn't worth the hassle, and it turned out they were right.

Grandpa Steve stayed single, and now that COVID was basically done and people were venturing out of their homes again—he was staying put.

Mid-December rolled around, and I was hunting online for gifts for my friends and family. But what the hell should I get for Papaw? I went online to find something—anything—for the guy I loved more than anyone in the universe, but I couldn't think of a damn thing. *What the fuck do you get for a man who never leaves his apartment? He doesn't like anything! He doesn't like anybody . . .*

Then it hit me. My whole life Grandpa Steve would ask me, "Matthew, when you gonna get me a girlfriend?" Well, I couldn't buy him one of those, but . . .

I have never hit *Add to Cart* so fast as when I found the pocket pussy.

Normally I would explain what a pocket pussy is, but if you're reading this book, you probably already know. Even if you don't . . . I mean, come on. The goddamn thing is called a "pocket pussy," and I was buying it for a dude who never got laid. Figure it out.

When I woke up on Christmas morning in Ohio, I was so fucking excited I could hardly get through our usual holiday breakfast of blueberry waffles, bacon, and Bud Lights. Papaw had been through four or five of those by eight a.m. My family knew what I got him, so we spent the morning giving each other the side-eye and holding back laughs. He was used to getting socks, maybe a pair of jeans, or a sleeve of Copenhagen Long Cut, because it's all he fucking asked for. We couldn't wait for him to open this very different kind of gift, throw it to the floor, and angrily announce in his best cranky old-man voice, "What the fuck is this shit?!"

Finally, the moment arrived. The whole room went silent. I handed him his gift, terribly packaged with what Dollar General calls wrapping paper, ready for my grandpa to melt my face with a hot blast of profanity—and what does this motherfucker do?

"Thank you," the man says, with this sickeningly earnest look on his face. "This is exactly what I needed."

We all burst with laughter. I couldn't believe it. Like, this is exactly what you needed?! It's a Fleshlight, not a Purple Heart, man. Relax, and stop feeling so honored.

So yeah—he loved it. And that year I got no greater gift than watching a sixty-year-old curmudgeon unwrap a 3D-printed vagina. I'll never forget the smile that took over his face and his patented inhale-laugh when he opened it. Over the years I'd bought him a guitar, new boots, and even a new TV, but I knew *this* was his favorite. I had finally found him the perfect girlfriend. Who would've guessed she was only $140 and made in China? I guess I was lucky—most people's crotchety old grandparents can't stand "the Orientals."

Fast-forward to February. I hadn't spoken to my grandpa since Christmas. So I called him up. "STEEEEEEEVE! How you doing, man? I love you. I miss you. Christmas was fun, always good to spend the holidays with you." I'm holding the phone, standing there with a shit-eating grin on my face, knowing he's had two solid months with my present. How exactly do you transition from "I love you" to "Pretty sick fake pussy, huh?" So I take a deep breath and sheepishly ask, "How was it?"

There was just silence on his end of the phone. "Are you using it RIGHT NOW? Like, fucking answer me, dawg! What's the review? I'm interested."

He goes, "No no no no no." He's getting all defensive. And I will never forget these next words for as long as I live. He says, "No, no, no, no . . . I, uh . . . I broke her neck."

There is SO much to unpack in that one sentence. First of all . . . *her?!* You gave it a pronoun. Now it's real. Second . . . *neck?!* That's not even what body part it is! And third . . . *you broke it?* Man, how hard are you going? Fifteen years and you forget how to be a gentleman?!

Fast-forward again to the following Christmas. I'm getting ready to go back to Ohio. I'm finishing up shopping for my family, and again, it comes down to him. Now I'm really struggling. *What the fuck do I get him? How do I possibly top what I did last year?*

Clearly he enjoyed the last one. And my man hasn't had any pussy since at least February. Because, you know, he apparently broke it. So I do what any decent, thoughtful grandson would do in this situation. I double down and decide to get him another one. I'm gonna make it two pocket pussies, two Christmases in a row.

I am grandson of the decade, easily.

Obviously, I was a little bit more aware of what it was going to be put through this time around, so I'd have to find him a more durable one. Something with a stronger . . . neck.

I'm at home, doing my homework, on a quest to find the Bentley of pocket pussies. A pocket pussy with traps—trying to find my papaw a Trap Queen for Christmas. But I couldn't find exactly what I was looking for. Surely he'd pop a blow-up doll if he was shattering hardware. Then, right when I was about to give up, I found it.

I was out on tour and, as luck would have it, I was performing near an adult store. I, uh, had to use the bathroom. So I went inside, and right near the register what do I see but the latest version of my grandpa's ex.

We are talking a *next-level* pocket pussy. I've never seen anything like it—and I'd done a lot of research. Like, a lot. For my grandpa. This lady was all souped up, with all these different modes and even machine washable (I know) material. It came with different attachments and parts. It was a real Swiss Army pussy. Like this thing had a compass and a can opener. It could've doubled as a canteen if you got lost in the woods.

But by far the best attachment it came with was a suction cup. The idea being you can fucking stick this thing to a wall. I mean, obviously. Like, how did no one think of this before? So you could switch positions. Or maybe you wanna work your legs? Whatever you want to add to your repertoire, you can do it.

I was sincerely impressed, like, *This is so creative! Now Papaw's got free roam of the house. He's not bed bound, beating his dick like a pilgrim! He's got options!*

I was excited for him, but also fucking terrified that I'd go home next time to possibly find chunks of dry wall—at waist level—missing all around his place. Like, doing a bit of remodeling, are we? Is this project mid-demo? Or did you literally fuck from the window to the wall? Got your dick sucked down the hall.

Oh, Steve. Steve, Steve, Steve, Steve, Steve.

My fans naturally started to get to know my grandpa Steve, too.

I mean, not as well as "she" did, thank God. But still. I didn't just have Papaw help open my *Only Fans* special. I talked about him onstage all the time, too. Hell, the first time I ever told the story about him and the Pocket Pussy from Christmas was on my buddy Adam Ray's podcast. When someone becomes a die-hard fan, when you're a real one, it's like you're more than just a part of the audience. You're a part of my family.

Think about it. People who had been following me since the very beginning—and, you know, there were maybe four or five—had literally watched me growing up. They'd seen me get new teeth. They'd watched me hit puberty at a ridiculously late age. They'd heard me tell stories about my home, my high school, and my grandpa. They'd been with me through all the ups and downs. And unfortunately, every family does have its share of downs.

Sometimes so far down that shit hits rock bottom.

In the middle of 2022, I started noticing that something about Grandpa Steve seemed . . . off. He was coughing a bunch, mentioning pains in his chest. He'd never been a particularly heavy guy, but all of a sudden he was getting downright skinny. I mean straight-up gaunt. Whenever he and I talked, for as grumpy as he could be, he always had a smile for me. But now his energy was flagging. He seemed tired all the time, worn down. It reminded me a little of what I'd been like when I was fighting my depression during the pandemic.

Papaw was deteriorating, but I tried to put it out of my mind. Like, maybe if I just pretended everything was cool, it really *would be* cool. Then one day he gave me a call. He gave me the news in his own way—there were no hysterics, nothing dramatic. Even when my grandpa bitched about stuff—and he bitched about everything, all the time—he just wanted to vent. He never wanted people to feel sorry for him. Complaining was his official love language. He kept it simple, cut right to the facts.

"Yeah, so, I ain't been feeling too good, as you may have noticed, so I went and got myself checked out. The doc told me I got cancer."

Despite it all, I was still in disbelief. "Jesus, Papaw. Are they sure?"

"Sure as sure can be," he said. "All I'm waiting on is what stage it is. How bad it's spread."

This might sound crazy, but even after that I kept my hopes up. I don't know. I guess when you're working in something as unreliable as comedy, you learn to tell yourself whatever you need to hear to keep going. Or maybe he'd been such a rock for me that I couldn't even imagine living without him. Maybe for once I figured it was my turn to be strong for him.

"Don't worry, Papaw," I told him over and over again. "People are coming up with new cures for this shit every single day. Do you know how much money they pour into this research? You can fight this thing! I know you can!"

And he did. Or at least he tried. But sometimes fighting the good fight—even fighting the best fight—isn't good enough.

On November 28, 2022, only a couple months after he called to tell me he had cancer, Papaw died. It happened so fucking fast, I couldn't believe it. But this was a reality even I couldn't deny. The universe—whether that's cosmic energy or the angels looking out for us or crazy-ass luck, whatever you want to call it—had been swinging my way so much recently. The insane viral success of the "Lazy Hero" video had pulled me back from the brink of giving up on comedy forever. But I guess sometimes the universe just tells you to fuck off.

My grandpa passed just two and a half weeks before I was scheduled to film my second self-produced special. It was weird, because I had already been planning on making my new special my greatest tribute to him ever. No more FaceTiming with my dude for a fun little sketch before the show. Nope, now that I could afford it, I was gonna fly Papaw down to Austin for the shoot so I could thank him in front of the sold-out crowd for everything he'd done for me. I wanted *him* to take a bow in front of all the people his love and support had brought together under one roof.

But now that he was gone, what was I supposed to do? Yeah, my career was finally taking off. But what did it matter if I couldn't share it with the person I'd loved most in the world? How the fuck was I supposed to be funny when my heart was still raw and bleeding? How could I put on a goddamn comedy show when all I could do was cry?

I sat down, tried to clear my mind as best I could, and I thought about it. And look—I know this is basically a cliché, but it's the honest truth. I knew Grandpa Steve would've wanted me to go through with the show. Hell, this was a dude who'd thought there was nothing funnier than sitting down with his ten-year-old grandson to watch a movie about a filthy, foul-mouthed Santa Claus who liked to fuck in parking lots. To say my papaw had a dark sense of humor would pretty much qualify as the biggest understatement of all time.

So I decided to honor him the best way I knew how—by going even darker.

I started by naming the special after him, calling it *Matthew Steven Rife*. The "Steven" had come from him, so it only felt right. We highlighted Steven at the theater and lit it so it popped. I found a photo of him holding me as a baby and put it next to his favorite hat on a table under a dim spotlight on the corner of the stage. At the venue, I tracked down an old leather chair, a near perfect stand-in for his favorite recliner that he sat in every day, and placed it in the corner, stage left. I saved him a seat, the best one in the house, but it wasn't just for him—it was for me. I never pointed out any of the props to the audience, didn't really care if they noticed. I just wanted my papaw in the room. I wanted him close.

Best of all, I decided to open the show by telling my new favorite story. About Grandpa Steve and the Pocket Pussy Christmas Miracle.

I got through four unbelievable tapings of my special. And in the grand finale of my final show, I took a moment to explain to the crowd that the incredible man I'd gifted a pocket pussy to had passed away just a couple weeks prior. My fans—my second family—listened as I talked about my grandpa Steve and what he meant to me. Then, from behind the leather chair, I pulled out another pocket pussy, gave a toast to the heavens, and poured out the ashes of my deceased grandpa from his favorite sex toy.

The audience lost their shit. Waves of applause, laughter, and— yes—shock. Like, *Did Matt Rife just . . . ?*

Yes. Yes, I did.

Relax, it was kitty litter.

Before he died, my grandpa Steve actually told me—no joke—that he'd leave the second, souped-up pocket pussy for me in his will. And let me tell you—you have never had an awkward conversation until you've had to ask an estate attorney if you're the heir to a top-of-the-line Fleshlight.

"Um," I said, "I'm interested for . . . sentimental purposes."

"Right," he answered. "Let me get back to you on that."

I'm still waiting for that call. And I hope he does get back to me. Cuz I'll take that pocket pussy, put Grandpas Steve's ashes in it, name it Ashley, and then *I'll* fuck it.

Just keepin' it in the family.

15

MILF & COOKIES

I walked onto the stage at the club in Des Moines, Iowa, ready to do what any sane person visiting Des Moines, Iowa, for the very first time would do—absolutely, mercilessly *destroy* Des Moines, Iowa.

Come on, y'all. Can you really blame me?

Unless you work in cows or corn, traveling to the heart of the Midwest usually isn't a highlight in anyone's career. These places are called flyover states for a reason. Because pretty much the only thing they're good for is flying over them. Ideally far over the clouds, miles above, while you're watching *Avengers* on the plane's entertainment system for the twentieth time because what else the fuck are you gonna do? Count the quilt patchwork of fields below?

When I first started performing around the country, I was all about hitting the big exciting cities, and that usually meant the coasts. New York, Los Angeles, San Francisco, Boston, Philly, whatever. Not just because that was the fastest way to reach the most people in the biggest crowds, but because, you know, there was actually shit to *do* there in my few minutes of free time. Concerts and sports to check out, high-end shopping to get done, history museums and fine art exhibits to visit and critique.

And don't you *dare* question my passion for history museums and the fine arts. I am an absolute aficionado when it comes to lyrical tramp stamps and war memorials.

Besides, I had spent most of my life stuck in Ohio. I figured I already knew what all these towns had to offer—the pizza place, the gas station, the pizza place in the back of the gas station. What sight was I supposed to get excited about seeing when I plopped down for a comedy show literally being staged on a stack of hay underneath the single stop light? *Hey Matt, the dude down the road's got his very own meth lab in the basement! I heard he just branched out into fentanyl, too. And they say we don't got culture!*

But you know what? That night in April of 2023, the town of Des Moines, Iowa, was gonna do its very best to prove me wrong. Me, Matt Rife—who's generally only wrong about basically everything 86 percent of the time, which is actually a pretty good track record compared to most people in entertainment.

I went up in front of the audience of three hundred people and got about ten minutes into verbally bullying everything it meant

to live and die in Iowa when suddenly a soft voice from the crowd broke in.

"You seem stressed," someone was saying. "I thought maybe a gift would help."

I scanned the first few rows in the club. The first thing I noticed was just how happy everyone was to be there. One thing I'd started to realize about all the big cities was that the audiences tended to have a cynical, "been there, done that" vibe. They had a million places to go, a million things to see, and I just happened to be one of them. But that wasn't the case with a smaller Midwestern crowd. I was giving these guys shit, and what were they giving me? Warm, appreciative smiles. They had saved up for this night, this was something special, and I could feel it.

The next thing I noticed was her. The owner of that soft sultry voice. She was blond, she was curvaceous, she was stunning, and she was in her forties—and I *know* you know I've got a type. Best of all, she had started walking up to the stage with a big, sexy smile on her face because she wanted to give me . . . a gift.

A gift?

I shit you not, all I could think in the moment was, *This fine-ass cougar is seriously about to give me head. Now. In front of everyone. In Iowa.*

Because that would've been the best gift, obviously.

And I was quite literally there for it. I would've kicked everyone in that crowd out of the room. Or let them watch, I didn't care.

———

The nameless MILF was right—I really was stressed.

Like, *Very perceptive of you, hot lady who's about to go down on me up onstage in the middle of my show. You're a natural empath. A real people-person.*

On the surface, nothing could've been better. A few months prior, I'd released my special *Matthew Steven Rife* on YouTube, and it already had a few million views. That didn't just mean I had a bunch of new comedy fans, it also meant that millions of people knew just how fucking awesome my grandpa Steve was—and that was by far most important to me.

I was also on the first leg of my very first big national tour, which I was calling my Chipped Shoulder Tour. This is gonna sound corny as hell, y'all, but this was my fucking dream. Me, Matt Rife—headlining a tour with my name at the top of the bill, getting paid to do an hour of comedy in front of real live, breathing human beings with an actual pulse. I was performing at cities all over the country—and yes, whatever you might think, Des Moines does actually count as a city. I was performing at clubs that had never even considered having me before. *And* I was able to bring my buddies along with me to open for me, manage the logistics, and take photos.

Think about it—how many times do you scan the lineup of your local comedy club, and you barely even recognize any of the names? Well, until ridiculously recently, that had been me—just another comic stuck in the grind, trying to make a buck. Now, all of a sudden, I felt like a real, honest-to-God, successful working

comedian for the first time in my life. This was why I had left high school early, this was why I had let Gary Abdo throw tennis balls at my nuts onstage, this was why I'd moved to LA and taken the bus all over town, sitting next to pissing homeless people. To achieve exactly this. My own tour. And it felt great.

But at the same time, I was calling it the Chipped Shoulder Tour for a reason—that famous chip on my shoulder was only getting bigger. Yes, I was finally getting gigs at clubs I'd been hitting up for years, but they were still only giving me the crumbs off their table. Like, "Sure, we can give Matt a night . . . on our *emptiest weekend* all year. Let's see if he can get some of his TikTok fans to show up, because we damn well ain't gonna do shit to promote him. Good luck!"

And it wasn't just the clubs that weren't giving me the respect I'd earned. TV networks, movie studios, streamers—none of them were fucking with me. Hell, I was still putting out my own stuff on YouTube! None of the big boys wanted to even *think* about giving me a movie or a TV show. As far as they were concerned, with social media fame you were "meh" until proven undeniable. They simply didn't believe that my internet fans would show up on other platforms. "Yeah, he's big on TikTok," they'd say, "but TikTok isn't Peacock or Paramount Plus."

Yeah, right—I guess because people actually watch TikTok, huh?

But what got me more than that—more than anything put together—was this bizarre reputation that people had already pegged me with, literally *weeks* after anyone had even started learning my name. You're reading this book, so you've probably heard this before. Trust me, I hear it about a million times a day: "He's too young, he won't sell tickets, he only does crowd work, not 'real comedy'—and he looks like he'd be an asshole."

The "young" thing I've been hearing since I was born, because even before I started comedy, I looked younger than my age. Not hitting puberty until you're twenty-two years old does tend to hit you with a label. And the bias against crowd work is a really old, tired cliché in the comedy community. There's this belief that "respectable comics" should practice and perfect every beat of their routine before they go onstage, and that talking to your audience is a lazy way of avoiding all the work that goes into honing a well-crafted set.

First off—honing a well-crafted set? That's exactly what I do, and you can see it in any of my specials. The crowd work stuff is seriously one percent of my act—it just happens to be the most famous one percent because the clips are short, easy to watch, and no one had seen this kind of crowd work before. Second— *lazy*? Have you ever actually tried to make an entirely improvised, five-minute-long conversation with a complete stranger not just interesting but *funny*? I'm not talking about getting a single laugh and moving on. I'm talking about a sustained build with multiple reveals and misdirections, all peaking at exactly the right moment. I have to listen, I have to think on my feet, I have to stay entirely in the moment while simultaneously staying three steps ahead—and

I have to make it look easy. Because rule number one is to never, ever look forced or inauthentic. Trust me—if it actually was easy, a hell of a lot more people would be doing it.

But the asshole label—that's the one I really straight-up do not get.

You know the whole thing about being too young? Well, when you spend most of your life being scrawny, with a high-pitched voice and fucked-up little Tic Tac teeth, you learn how to be self-deprecating. Fast. It's kind of like the ugly-person's version of playing dead. Like, "If I crack jokes about how messed up I look first, maybe everyone else will just forget about making fun of me and move along. If I'm really lucky, maybe I'll get a laugh out of it, too."

Self-deprecation is my bread and butter. You can see it in all my comedy, from back when every other joke in *Wild 'N Out* is about how I look like Bieber with an extra chromosome. Even now that I look like a high-priced trailer-park fuckboy . . . all I ever do is make fun of the fact that I look like a high-priced trailer-park fuckboy.

Do I roast people when I'm up onstage? Yes, to a crisp. I'm a comic, that's what we do. And for me, a clever, well-timed roast isn't an insult, it's the opposite. It's my love language. Roasting my friends—and getting roasted by them—has always been how we show each other we care. That might sound screwed up to you—and maybe it is, what the hell do I know—but think about it. True friendship is about being vulnerable with someone, right? What better way to show vulnerability than to say, "Yo, that thing you're insecure about that you try so hard to hide? We actually love you for it. It's what makes you *you*. And yes . . . your hair-line is definitely terrified of your forehead." That's why my crowd work interactions never feel hostile. Why we always have so much fun bantering. It's because my crowd understands that me fuck-ing with them is just my way of showing affection. They know my deepest, darkest secret, which is that I'm actually a pretty nice guy.

I say please, I say thank you, I say bless you when other people sneeze. Unless you're one of these elbow sneezers who don't have the common courtesy to at least sneeze into their fucking shirt. I'll see you in hell, assholes. I've got manners and I think your mom's gonna love me. And if I have anything to say about it, I'll tuck my napkin in my shirt when it's time to eat her for dessert. Now go to bed, I'm starving.

Why the label, then? My best theory, my only guess, is that a lot of dudes in our industry are insecure. Comedy is one of the few art forms where it's not cool to be cool. Comedians are by nature a weird bunch. We're misfits. We're horseflies. We're annoying as fuck. No one tries to be funny because they're already popular and well-liked. Hell, like I just said—*I* only wanted to be funny because I started out feeling like such a freak. So maybe when some people in our business see a young fuckboy who's successful doing some-thing that's supposed to be reserved for the uncool—maybe that's triggering. Maybe the first place they go is "looks like an asshole." Whatever. I seriously don't know. But go ahead, call me conceited and prove my point.

All I can really say is—it pisses me off. But in a very polite, non-asshole-ish way. It turns my chip into the size of a great fucking oak, and I carry that thing with me wherever I go. Even up onstage. And especially during my first-ever national tour, when all I really, desperately wanted was to prove all the haters wrong.

So yes, random hot MILF in the audience in Des Moines, Iowa, as much as I want to entertain you, I probably do look a bit stressed right now. And yes, I will very happily, very humbly, very gratefully accept that BJ to help me relax.

Thank you very much. God bless you while we're at it.

Where's my napkin?

Okay, it turns out she wasn't offering me a BJ.

Damn.

Instead, she was headed up to stage with this mysterious sparkly bag. After I got over the painful realization that I was not about to get head from this gorgeous lady, the first thing I thought was *Should I call security?* And then I thought, *Motherfucker—it's gonna be another Build-A-Bear.*

In case you live under a very slimy rock or are extremely poor with context clues, a Build-A-Bear is exactly that—you buy this cuddly, delightful stuffed bear that you dress up and accessorize to make it feel more personal. Well, back in those days, pretty much anytime anyone was nice enough to bring me a gift, it was a Build-A-Bear. This was because of a Red Flag interaction I had at a show in Florida, where a girl complained a guy bought her a Build-A-Bear on a second date and that was a red flag. This ungrateful teddy hater made it into an online clip, obviously.

The clip goes viral, and the next thing I know I'm getting *swamped* by these creepy-ass bears at every show. Which would've been cool, except *no one* put any thought into these goddamn Build-A-Bears! I mean, that's the whole point, right? You personalize them! You make them unique! But chicks would hand me these bears, and half of them didn't have on any clothes at all—which, point taken, some people look better naked. But still—*lazy!* If I got lucky, they were maybe wearing a pair of pants and sunglasses. I got a firefighter once, and that only made me feel like a failure because all I do is tell jokes. And one time, soon after Grandpa Steve died, a lady brought me a bear that was entirely decked out like an admiral in the navy. I'm talking a dapper little hat, a bunch of medals pinned to his uniform, even a name tag that said "Steve."

Okay, that one was actually pretty cool. Bravo, Ma'am. Papaw would've been touched.

But the rest of them? All the nudist Build-A-Bears who had God knows what on their mind? I had a billion of them, and I had no interest in luring kids into a creepy van during my spare time, so I donated them to a family services charity in LA. My apologies for the lack of shirts.

And Build-A-Bears were actually one of the more, uh, appropriate gifts. After my *Matthew Steven Rife* special, what other than

the navy was my papaw associated with? That's right—pocket pussies. So I promptly received dozens of them. Now, the free Flesh-
lights actually did come in handy. What was I supposed to do? The
charity wouldn't take those! The road is lonely, shut up.

Two other women got me dildos. That one's a puzzler. Never
done any bits about dildos. Definitely no viral clips (that I know of)
of me and dildos. In fact, I honestly don't think I've even typed the
word "dildos" until right now. To my knowledge these two women
didn't know each other, had never spoken to each other, they lived
in separate states, attended entirely different shows, but somehow
both of them looked at me and came to the exact same conclusion:
this man needs a dildo. I don't love that I give off that *vibe*.

Oh, and one time someone left me a nice clean pair of socks.

So this kind-hearted MILF handed me the mysterious sparkly
bag, sat back down in the second row with her girlfriends, and I
peeked inside. Waiting for me was something better than Build-A-
Bears and sex toys and socks put together. Hell, it was even better
than a blow job, and I am not making that up.

She'd baked me cookies.

Homemade chocolate chip, in a Tupperware container. Or, as
they call them in Iowa, "the good dishes." And let's be clear—not
all chocolate chip cookies are created equal. I actually had a fan
bring me cookies before—I mean, I've gotten socks and dildos,
so this shouldn't come as a surprise. They were trash. Obviously I
smiled and said thanks and I pretended that they were really good,
but she'd burned them and they were extra crispy. Apparently,

some people actually like their cookies crispy, and those people are psychotic and should never be trusted. About anything.

But these cookies were flawless. Cooked all the way through, so no undercooked salmonella, but still somehow also soft and chewy. And with them in the bag is a red tee that says, "I went to Iowa and all I got was this T-shirt and a BLOW JOB."

As cheeky as the shirt was, the cookies were fucking fire! The blow job was gonna have a hard time beating this. But who says this has to be an either-or situation?

"Thank you so much," I say into the mic. "What's your name?"

"Christina," she says with a sexy smile.

"She's a *grandma!*" one of her cockblocking friends chimes in.

It drops like a bomb. Like, are you fucking kidding me? A grandma? I'm ready to put the shower chair to use—and if I *do* blow her back out, at least I know she has a heating pad, some Icy Hot, and a decent chiropractor. There's already plastic on the furniture—we could make a mess all over the throw pillows and cleanup would be a breeze.

Suddenly, as far as I'm concerned, this just went from being a comedy bit to being a very intimate first date. Which just happens to be taking place in front of three hundred people who are enjoying every single second.

"How old are you?" I ask her as I take another bite of her amazing cookies. She shakes her head, embarrassed. "Say it . . . *Say it.*"

More shaking her head. More embarrassment.

"This is dirty talk to me. Come on." She's. My. Type.

"Forty-five," she finally admits coyly. Perfect. Although if I'm being honest, fifty would be even more of a turn-on.

Christina had just gotten divorced. "Men of Iowa, seriously, what the fuck is wrong with you? Morons! Do you not see a diamond in the haystack??" Maybe that's not the saying, but the majority of my blood wasn't in my brain. I take another bite of that incredible cookie, and I notice her look at something on her phone.

"What's that?" I say. "What is it?"

She shows me and my eyes open wide.

"Is that your *daughter*??"

Y'all, let me tell you—this is absolutely a case of like mother, like daughter. If I spotted Christina and her twenty-one-year-old daughter Maggie together at Applebee's, the SoHo House of Des Moines, I absolutely would assume they're sisters. They look identical.

"Shit," I say, taking another bite. "This is about to be the most uncomfortable Thanksgiving ever. Because if you taste this good, this is gonna be a *problem*."

Christina hands me her phone and I smile. "Let's swipe out of Instagram, see what else is in here. Let's go through a photo album."

"No!" Christina says. "Wait!"

The audience *explodes*. And between me and you, I wanted to scroll. I wanted to so bad. But respectfully—and regretfully—I did not.

Instead I do something even better. Turns out Christina's daughter Maggie is in college in Jacksonville, Florida—that's where

Harvard is, right?—and I decide to FaceTime her right then and there. Onstage. And miraculously she answers.

"Maggie, that is not your angle," I say. "Where are you right now?"

"Hungover as *shit!*" she says.

Amazing. Jacksonville truly is a world capital for scholars. Maggie must be pulling all-nighters to meet those incredible academic demands.

Honestly, by this point I'm feeling our banter has reached its natural conclusion. Yes, I need to finish these cookies. Obviously I need to ponder the T-shirt and its rather profound message to me. And most pressingly, I need to debate who I'm gonna ask out first—Christina or her daughter. (Really no debate. Like I said . . . the type.) But all of this can easily take place after the show.

Then, right after I hand Christina back her phone, I suddenly get interrupted by the most unique heckler I've ever encountered in all my years of stand-up.

Her tits squeak.

You read that right. Christina's perfect yet fake titties actually *squeaked* during my set.

"What was that?" I ask, stunned.

"That was my tits," she says.

No joke, my jaw literally drops. "You're lying. That did not just happen."

Except it did. And then it happens again.

SQUEEEAK!

The crowd goes batshit crazy. Honestly, so do I.

"She has a *squeaky toy* in her titties!" I announce. "And you talkin' to a *dawg*. WOOF!"

I thought about Christina's kids who were lucky enough to breastfeed. Because y'all know what goes great with cookies, right? Milk. And silicon.

My "date" with Christina didn't just end up being a good time—though I swear she did not help me earn that T-shirt after the show—it also made the "Lazy Hero" video look, well, lazy. Sorry, all you paramedics out there. The edited-down clip swept across every platform I had, getting over 100 million views across TikTok, Instagram, FaceTime, and Twitter.

Christina had fun with it, too. She used her perfect cookie recipe to raise money for a local charity, and she gained hundreds of thousands of followers on her own platforms, where people know her as "THEE TikTok MILF," that's the "Mom I'd Like to Follow." And of course, both she and Maggie now have OnlyFans accounts, because at this point it feels like almost every girl in America is practically required to get one when they turn eighteen. What can I say, man—that's the world we live in. I don't have a subscription to either of them—but you absolutely should. Through the entire experience, Christina has been humble, charismatic, and as beautiful on the inside as she is on the outside.

Videos like "MILF & Cookies" don't come along often. Hell, they come along almost never. You're lucky if a crowd interaction goes longer than a minute. Five minutes is a blessing. But to get forty-five minutes of joke after joke and ridiculous reveals and—yes—tits that *squeak*? That's a goddamn miracle of personal chemistry, quick thinking, and serendipity. But that's kind of the point of creating something special, right? If it was easy, it wouldn't be so special anymore.

People always ask me what the specific moment was when I finally broke through and became a legit comedy star. And the truth is there wasn't one. It happened over a couple years, not overnight. But slowly and surely, as the viral videos piled up, as my crowd interactions and the TikTok algorithm worked their mysterious magic, my career gained a momentum that was literally undeniable.

Some of the gatekeepers of comedy and entertainment finally started opening their arms to me, and it wasn't long before I launched a new tour that would change everything, taking my comedy to a level I can still barely comprehend.

The T-shirt Christina gave me was wrong in the end. I got almost everything I'd ever dreamed of during that stop in Iowa—*except* a blow job.

But, you know, I'll be back next year.

16

STROKING THE GENIE

I hold an ancient genie lamp gently in my strong and sizable hands. Gently, I begin to stroke its long, slender, uh . . . beak? (Honestly, no idea what it's called. It's a fucking genie lamp.)

Faster. Faster. *Faster.*

FASTER!

When suddenly I hear this deep, steady breathing. And a climax.

"*Hey-hey! Atta boy!*" Ashton Kutcher pants, his head twitching. "Thanks for the dry rub, pal. It's not a fucking barbecue."

Apparently, I just made my teenage idol bust his nut. Not too shabby for a comic fuckboy trying to summon his very first magic genie. I didn't even care that he'd sternly declined wearing a turban, a black goatee, and blue body paint.

It was the summer of 2023, and I was supposed to be asking Ashton Kutcher—yes, *the* Ashton Kutcher—to grant me one wish, but it kinda felt like my biggest wishes were already being granted. I was standing in the living room of my tastefully decorated mid-century modern home with a stunning view of Los Angeles. I was chilling with my new best friends Ashton and his wife, Mila Kunis, who just happened to be the stars of my favorite TV program of all time, *That '70s Show*. And I was pretending to jerk off a lamp. What more could a guy want?

Now granted, the house wasn't mine—about five miles away, my roommate and I lived in a two-bedroom apartment that was currently strewn with unopened Amazon boxes and half-packed suitcases. And granted, Ashton and Mila were really there on business, to help me shoot a promo video for my new ProbleMATTic Tour, and not just because they were cool as fuck—which, by the way, they were. I didn't even know for sure if Ashton had really orgasmed, because, you know what? He's just that great of an actor. (Or maybe I *do* know. Sorry, guys—some clips are just too hot to make it to outtakes.)

But in a weird way, the reality of the promo shoot was even better than any fantasy. I mean, just a year earlier—a single year!—I had been scrounging together as many one-night shows as I could in little clubs in random towns across the country. I'd needed to pass out free tickets like candy just to get a respectable audience at each stop.

Now? Now I was about to launch a tour with the backing of Live Nation, who's not only the biggest name in the business—

they're the only name. Like, Live Nation doesn't just do dinky clubs or even two-hundred-person venues—these guys do motherfucking *stadiums*. And they had offered me the chance to shoot pretty much whatever kind of promotional video I could think of. I just had to bring them an idea.

Which obviously was Ashton Kutcher playing an ancient magical genie who popped out of a rusty old genie lamp to grant me a wish, thanks to my killer wizarding skills.

Obviously.

I think I came up with the idea because simply working with Ashton was a dream unto itself, you know? *That '70s Show* hadn't just been my favorite watch because it was fucking hilarious with relatable funny characters—although it was all that—I loved it because of what it represented. The seventies to me felt like this bygone era when life was simpler, better. When all that mattered was hanging out with your friends, watching a little TV, smoking a little weed, and maybe putting on the occasional leisure suit with a butterfly collar. If a multi-cam crew happened to be off in the wings recording it all with a laugh track, all the better. As long as social media and internet trolls wouldn't be invented for another fifty years or so, I'd be good.

I, of course, wanted to be Kelso, Ashton's character. Hot and dumb. I was never that dumb or that hot, but what's life without aspirations?

Bizarrely, not only did Live Nation love my fever dream of a pitch, it also turned out that Ashton Kutcher was a shareholder in Live Nation. Which is yet another reason why it's really, really awesome to be Ashton Kutcher. There was no wrangling with lawyers or agents to get him involved, no red tape or pompous showbiz flexing—my dude just texted me one day and was like, "Hey, you wanna FaceTime with me and Mila?" and I cooly and professionally texted back "AHHHH!!! YES RIGHT NOW PLEASE AND I REALLY HOPE THIS ALL CAPS ISN'T TOO CREEPY AHHHH!!"

And it was on.

We ended the promo with my actual wish. My true, honest-to-God dream I'd had since I first tried comedy back as a little kid growing up in Ohio.

"I wish for a world tour bigger than anything I could've ever dreamed of. And I want it fully sold out, with people from across the world who just want to come out, have a good time, and laugh. Can you give me that?"

Live Nation certainly seemed to think I'd be able to pull it off. They were building a global tour, booking me over a year out in theaters that could hold up to six-thousand people. Six-thousand fucking people! We're talking hard ticket sales, with only my name on the marquee, and absolutely no chicken fingers being delivered during the show. These fuckers, these supposed experts in the business, thought that I, Matt Rife—who a year ago couldn't sell *seventy tickets* in Phoenix—would be able to *sell out* Radio City Music Hall. (Spoiler alert: We sold out six of those.)

I was only twenty-seven years old. I truly didn't think past next Thursday. I had no fucking clue if I could make this work.

By this point, my social media platforms were doing numbers that to this day I can't really comprehend.

Seriously. Every single video I posted on TikTok was getting an average of 10 million views. Think about it—just a few months earlier, I couldn't believe it when "Lazy Hero" passed its first million views. Now? I was getting one million views *per hour*. Again, there wasn't really a single thing that pushed me over the edge—it was just a matter of consistently posting new videos that my audience seemed to crave, generating more and more momentum. For a nine-month period, my videos were the biggest thing on TikTok. A global phenomenon.

Which is ironic, because I really do fucking hate social media—thank you, trolls—but according to Live Nation and the other entertainment gurus, that huge audience had created a lot of pent-up demand for a new tour, even though I had only started the Chipped Shoulder tour literally a half year prior.

That should've made me feel pretty good about things—and it's not like I felt bad. But there was a lot of uncertainty. Especially because I had finally wrapped up my most popular bit ever, the one that ignited my entire crowd work craze. The one that truly launched my comic career.

That's right. I had finally performed my final Red Flags number.

As much as I loved the concept, it was time. My Red Flags act had legitimately become a phenomenon. Night after night, show after show, recently jilted and almost always drunk women were always so game to shit on the men in their life. And I was always happy to egg 'em on, pick apart their hypocrisies, and maybe reveal a red flag about them, too. Either as two-minute stand-alone clips or edited into thirty-minute compilation cuts, the videos were insane, relatable, and fucking hilarious—and they had launched me into social media superstardom. But they were also starting to take over my entire show.

Women would come to my performances and scream out "Do red flags!" in the middle of my set like I was a goddamn jukebox. To be fair, a lot of my new fans from social media had never even been to a stand-up show. They seriously thought that my entire act was the same thing as a TikTok video—no more, no less. And to be clear, I loved the fact that I was introducing people to stand-up for the first time in their lives. Any comic would kill for that honor. But *you* try telling a joke when every time you deliver a punch line, Susan from Boise shouts out "Dirty car!" or "Firefighters!" . . . even though she chain-smokes in bed and doesn't know how to drive.

I decided to hold a funeral for Red Flags. My buddy Elton Castee came up with the idea for an entire special that was nothing but crowd work, nothing but Red Flags and more Red Flags. This would be insanely hard to do—what if I got stuck with a thousand women who shouted nothing but *"Doesn't eat ass!"* for a straight hour?—and to make it work, we'd need the perfect environment.

We'd need a city where relationships go to die. A mecca for bad tans, botched lip injections, bottle service, and boat hoes. Someplace scammy, someplace seedy, where NFT and Bitcoin passed as sound investments, and bachelorette parties fueled by Tito's & Soda ruled the nights. All carried along by an EDM beat.

That's right. We went to Miami.

This is gonna sound hard to believe, but I'd never even been there before. I just knew it by reputation. But lucky for us, that reputation is right on the money. Because Miami was exactly what we got. *Peak* Miami.

The very moment I stepped out onstage at the big show—seriously, before I could even start my act—this dude in the front row, who's probably already plastered out of his mind, just starts screaming at me. And I mean *screaming*. I know I'm encouraging audience engagement here, but I can't even understand a word you're saying right now. You can't be so damn loud and drunk that you prevent all the *other* loud and drunk people from having a good time.

Security comes to very politely, very professionally escort this man away, and he just loses it. "It's because I'm gay, isn't it!" he shouts. "It's because I'm gay!"

"What?!" I say. "I didn't even know you were gay."

Next thing I know, this dude's punching a security guard in the chest, he's on the ground kicking everything around him, he's shouting, "Get off me you fucking faggot!"

I'd never seen reversed homophobia.

Welcome to Miami, I guess.

Once we got through that drama, we got more—but this was exactly the right kind. The ladies in the crowd hit me with some high-quality red flags. We got a woman going after men's rights activists, which made me think she fucked Jordan Peterson. We got someone who hated dudes who were funnier than her, which made me seriously question why she was at a comedy show. We even got a chick hating on her Ivy League–educated ex who happened to wear flip-flops. Which mostly made me happy because I got to finally confess to the world that I actually like having socks on during sex.

Because first off, my feet are cold, and second off, I use them for traction. How you can possibly argue with that, I have no idea.

My favorite, though, was someone who shouted out, "Legos in the bedroom!"

My first response was to say, "Legos in the bedroom?" Because honestly, repeating the phrase gave me a second to process just how ridiculous it was. My mind was spinning, like, what is this man doing with Legos in his bedroom?! Seriously, I want you to conjure up the S&M dungeon of your nightmares and just *imagine* that dildo for a second.

But as ridiculous as it is, the last thing I want to do is say what everyone expects, right? Instead I go right at her. "He had a Lego village in his bedroom. Okay, so you don't fuck with architecture. Did you ever play with them? Ungrateful!"

After that, she did the work for me. Because—thank you, Miami—her "job" was trading crypto. "I wanna roast you," I said.

"But you're gonna be poor anyway." She judged a man with fake buildings while she played with fake money.

Sad but true, people. Sad but true.

The special, *Walking Red Flag*, which I made with tons of help from my boy Elton, was released in spring 2023. And even though it was one of my most DIY specials ever—we had one camera man (also Elton) doing everything, and our sound gear was shit—it ended up being a huge success, quickly surpassing E11EVEN million views. And if you don't get that last reference, I highly, highly recommend going to Miami and checking out the world's most over-the-top strip club. (I'd tell you the story about watching a girl queef up a goldfish, but I don't really wanna talk about my experience at Sea-Section World.)

But now, just a couple months later, on the brink of launching an absurdly ambitious global tour, I had to wonder—with my most popular bit officially retired, would my fans still turn out to see me? It sounds crazy, but think about it—the magic of my Red Flags routine had in a sense been almost entirely responsible for igniting my career. It had injected crack cocaine straight into the jugular of my fan base.

How would they respond now that I had very publicly killed it off?

Radio City Music Hall had six thousand seats. No one would give a shit if I "only" sold three thousand of them. Yeah, it was a huge number in a hugely competitive market, but the only thing people would remember was "Matt Rife not only didn't sell out the show—he barely managed to fill half the venue."

The night before the first day of presales for the ProbleMATTic Tour, I tried my best to get some sleep in my hotel. I was in New York City to do some last-minute press before the launch. Earlier that day, I'd arrived in Times Square just as my very first billboard went live—a thirty-by-fifty-foot photo of me, shirtless, towering six stories above the center of the modern universe. I'd chosen the image as an homage to the famous Jim Morrison pose, partly because my beloved grandpa Steve had first introduced me to the Doors years ago—and partly because I knew the shot would get people talking.

New York had been where I'd first had a taste of success as a young performer, with my brief but extremely luxurious stint on MTV's reboot of *TRL*. I'd lived in a penthouse, I'd had a private driver, and yes, I'd refereed at least one fake sumo fight. Shortly after that gig ended, I'd returned to the city completely humbled, dragging my suitcase through the snow and staying in a freezing hostel as I performed for free at comedy clubs.

Now I was back, and seemingly back on top—but for how long? As exhausted as I was, all I could do was toss and turn in the hotel bed. I mean, I have horrible insomnia in the best of times, but this was crazy. My mind was flooded with excitement, anticipation, and—the best friend of any creative person—huge amounts of self-doubt.

Was I finally going to prove to the world—and myself—that I was more than just an internet sensation? Or was I gonna prove all the haters right?

Fuck going shirtless, I thought. *I should've leaked a nude.*

———

The next morning, after getting approximately twenty minutes of decent sleep, I groggily pulled my sleep mask off my face, rolled over, and checked my phone.

BAM.

Dozens upon dozens of texts from my agents and manager, and they're all pretty much saying the same thing:

"Sold out in Chicago!"

"Sold out in New York!"

"Sold out in Nashville!"

I couldn't breathe. Which was usually a sign I was having a panic attack. But in this case I was feeling nothing but joy. Was this really happening? The presale tickets for my most dedicated fans had sold out in fifteen minutes. It's hard to know what to do when your life changes in a matter of seconds, but there was one thing I knew for sure . . .

"Hello, room service?" I said into the phone. "Yes, I'll have the thirty-five-dollar eggs, please."

I could afford to treat myself to breakfast in bed.

There was one more city I just had to check before this really felt real: Columbus, Ohio. Miles from the small trashy town where I'd grown up, and the home of the club where Grandpa Steve had taken me to perform in my very first open mic—and bought enough tickets so they'd allow me up onstage.

I clicked on the Live Nation app, and I had sold out all two-thousand seats of the Palace Theater. And the waitlist was over eighty thousand. *Eighty-thousand people?* I'm from Ohio, and even I didn't know that many people lived there. You could've fit my entire town into the Palace. But with a waitlist of eighty thousand, I could've practically filled the iconic Ohio State horseshoe stadium.

Closing my eyes, I said a prayer of thanks to Papaw. He would've been proud. I wished he was still alive to see this and be part of it, but as corny as it might sound, I knew he was out there and that his energy was somehow making all this possible.

Turned out I didn't have to worry about ending Red Flags. With all the demand, we ended up adding shows to every single original date, plus new cities along the way. We still sold out everything. Over six hundred thousand tickets sold in just forty-eight hours. And it only stopped there because *we* stopped there. My entire team, my agents, my manager, even Live Nation—we all had to take a moment to savor the fact that we were making history. We had raised the bar for what was possible for a touring comic. When it was all said and done, we ended up selling almost a million tickets for the ProbleMATTic Tour.

Now, I've been told that usually this kind of thank-you should go at the very end of a book—but fuck it. I didn't get where I am by following the rules. So I'd like to take a moment to thank you. Yes, you, reading this. My life forever changed because of you. Without your support, I'd still be praying for someone to let me make them laugh. You showed up, you showed out, and you made me the happiest person on the planet. It's all thanks to you.

And, of course, the wise genie who magically granted my biggest wish, and who very strangely bears a striking resemblance to Ashton Kutcher.

Though he did warn me at the end of the promo not to go out and get myself canceled.

Oh well. Nothing's perfect.

17

THE WITCHTOK NONTROVERSY

I gotta say—when I did my Netflix special *Natural Selection*, there were a few *other* jokes I thought might be an issue.

Like, I talked shit about a three-year-old. A three-year-old. And yeah, he was a super annoying three-year-old on a plane, but still— I can understand how it might be a little jarring to hear a grown man talk about caving in the sternum of a toddler, okay? I went after an overweight lady who talked shit to me on the internet. I said that as far as I was concerned, Michael Jackson looked like an Asian woman, which he does. But still. The rotting corpse of a musical child molester (allegedly) has a very vocal support community on TikTok.

So let's just say that as someone who's used to speaking his mind—and used to getting blowback for it—I had mentally prepared myself for some of the usual internet trolls to be, shall we say, triggered. But *this* one? *This* joke? *Really?*

Swear to God, I never saw it coming.

It was a Sunday morning in November 2023, just a couple days after Netflix had released my special. I woke up that day with no idea what to really expect. I mean, you're talking to a guy who'd had his entire life turned upside down by internet videos. *Internet videos*. I'd woken up to clips like the "Lazy Hero" and "MILF & Cookies" earning millions of views overnight, seemingly out of nowhere. Who the hell knew what weird-ass turn my life was gonna take next? No way it could be perfect forever, right? But I have to admit that when it came to *Natural Selection*, my hopes were running pretty high.

By this point I'd released three self-produced specials on YouTube, and since my crowd work clips had gone batshit viral on TikTok, all of them had gone on to rack up tens of millions of views. But Netflix? In the modern era, Netflix is the comedian's Holy Grail. It's not just that every massive name from Chris Rock to Dave Chappelle to Bill Burr has done one. Netflix's gigantic international reach can take you from being a decent-sized star in America to being a worldwide celebrity. Having a Netflix special both legitimizes you and has the potential to take your tour to a level that comedians couldn't even dream of before the advent of streaming. Kind of like doing a set for Johnny Carson back in the day—if that set also helped you sell out every stadium from London to Singapore to Sydney.

For most of my career, even after I took off on social media, Netflix, like all the other mainstream gatekeepers, had refused to fuck with me. And for the same old reasons pretty much—he's too young, his online success won't translate, he looks like an asshole. But just like all the other gatekeepers, the numbers I'd been putting up in my ProbleMATTic Tour were so ridiculous they just couldn't deny me anymore.

When Netflix finally caved—I mean judiciously chose to give me an opportunity—I couldn't wait to shoot my special and prove them and the world wrong about everything. Well, except maybe the asshole part. In a funny way, obviously.

The prep for the shoot had been pretty seamless.

I was about fifty dates into the ProbleMATTic Tour, so I was in ring-ready shape. This special was gonna be an hour-long set of structured material with absolutely *no* crowd work. I knew I was taking a risk, because obviously I was famous for my audience interactions—some people *only* knew me as the crowd work guy—but what the fuck is life without taking a few risks? I wanted to give people something new, something fresh. In reality, crowd work was just a tiny percentage of my act. This was my chance to show everyone what I could do—and what I'd *been* doing since I started as a stand-up.

After going through a few potential directors who didn't quite fit, I contacted one of my oldest friends and mentors in the business—Erik Griffin, who'd first challenged me to be a funnier comic while also letting me crash on his couch in LA. I was halfway through my pitch when he cut me off midsentence. "Say less," he said. "I'm in." For the venue, I decided to go for pure audacity—Constitution Hall in Washington, D.C. I'd be surrounded by the nation's most historic monuments and performing on a stage that had hosted some of the biggest events of all time. Not only Eddie Murphy's *Delirious*, possibly the most magnificent special ever, but shows headlining James Brown, George Carlin, Richard Pryor, Elton John, a handful of presidents, and now . . . some kid from Bumfuck, Ohio.

Everything about the production was bigger and more elaborate than anything I had been a part of before. From the size of the technical crew to the number of cameras to the quality of the fucking craft-service food. I kept telling myself to treat this show just like any other, and in a sense it was. The day of the first shoot—we were filming four shows to get all the material we needed—I had the same routine as always. Wake up, hit the gym, write and have lunch, head to the venue around five p.m. for sound check, play a little music in the greenroom, and chop it up with the boys to warm up our silly. There was a seven p.m. curtain on a two-show night, then a meet and greet, then reset for the late show. Like clockwork.

But who the hell was I kidding? This was the biggest show of my uncomfortably young life! Everyone I knew from basically everything was there—friends, family, you name it. Not to mention the execs from Netflix and Live Nation who were all there to judge—I mean support—me as my dream came true. No pressure!

All I can say is . . . thank God I had more than one show to get it right. Night one went well, but I still had some nerves. The audience probably didn't notice, but watching the playback, I did. My energy felt just a *tiny bit* tight, my timing was just a *hair* off. But Erik proved to be the perfect director. We reviewed the footage, he suggested some adjustments, and on night two I fucking nailed it.

Had I been confident before the show? Yes. Cocky? Absolutely. But was I currently relieved as hell that I'd actually delivered? You're goddamn right I was.

When I saw the final edit of the show—which Erik, the editor, and I worked on like crazy—I was amazed at how good it looked. But the final product that ended up on Netflix was *not* the final approved pass that Erik and I signed off on. I wasn't a fan of the jumpy cuts that had been added in the beginning. How something like that happens after final approval, I don't know. It's my only true gripe with the special. Nevertheless, I had never filmed anything so beautiful. Did it capture the energy of one of my live shows? Not exactly. But Netflix's international audience expected a certain level of polish, and *Natural Selection* had polish spewing out of every available orifice. That, and class.

The day of the special's release, it all seemed to be paying off. Totally coincidentally Netflix was, at that exact moment, moving to a new era of data transparency and sharing rankings. So you can actually see the rankings of popular shows on the platform in real time.

And we were opening at number one. In over forty different countries!

Our whole team was on a rocket ship. You never take being at the top for granted—hell, I'd literally been on the verge of quitting the business *only a year earlier*—but the special seemed like it was taking off. Friday night was ebullient. Saturday, transcendent. And then came Sunday morning.

I looked at my phone, read my mentions, saw the headlines, and it felt like everything came crashing down.

If you're reading this book, chances are you remember what I like to refer to as The Joke:

"My friend and I went into a diner and the hostess had a black eye. He said, 'Damn, I feel like they should put her in the kitchen or something where no one can see her,' and I said, 'I feel like if she could cook . . . she wouldn't have that black eye.'"

Cue the audience: A surprised flood of "whoooaaa" laughter, like *Can I laugh at this?* But they do. A lot. And now they're ready for more.

These few lines are what I opened my show with. To me, The Joke was just that—a joke. I wasn't trying to make some kind of profound statement about the state of our society. I was trying to set the tone for the rest of the show via a personal spin on a classic joke. I like dark humor, and there was more of it to come. Mission accomplished, right? Apparently not. Because the internet responded to those few simple lines like I'd planted a nuclear bomb at the center of the Earth and blown us all to hell. *Matt Rife built his audience on women and turned on them right away! Matt Rife condones domestic violence! Matt Rife is a handsome Squidward!* And my personal favorite: *Matt Rife is a MENACE to society!*

You want to know the funniest part? The Joke wasn't actually what generated the most outrage. No, what burned people most was the gag I followed it up with: "Of course I felt bad for her, but she should have had her protection crystals."

I shit you not, this line seemed to be just as upsetting to women as my supposed support for domestic violence. And by "women" I mean upper-middle-class ladies who literally collect gravel and were apparently so, so, SO angry that I don't believe in astrology.

Practically overnight I had gone from being an internationally beloved darling of the internet to being, in certain circles at least, basically canceled, and certainly reviled. I learned very fast that what TikTok giveth, TikTok can taketh away. Or in this case— WitchTok.

What exactly do I mean by "WitchTok"? I'm happy you asked!

Let's start by giving all my critics the benefit of the doubt— which, by the way, is something they absolutely do not deserve— and actually assume that they're making their argument in good faith. Something along the lines of "Matt Rife made a joke we found offensive, therefore he advocates the beating of women."

The idea that simply because I made a joke about domestic violence means that I somehow support domestic violence is on its face—so to speak—clinically insane. Comedy doesn't exist to make you feel comfortable, it exists to challenge you, to make you squirm in your seat, and, yes, to make you laugh. Some of the greatest comedians of all time—from Lenny Bruce to Sam Kinison to Bill Burr—were or still are masters of the art of offense. Now, maybe you didn't find The Joke funny. Maybe it wasn't to your taste. That's fine. That happens. Not to me very often—but it happens.

But that doesn't make me a supporter of domestic violence. I mean, Jesus—I grew up with an abusive stepdad. Verbal abuse, psychological abuse, physical abuse—I experienced it all. Half the reason I spent every weekend with my grandpa Steve was to get away from it, to find someplace safe. Not only do I not condone violence, I despise it. That's part of why I wanted to joke about it— to defuse that trauma. When me and my friends are roasting each other, are we *trying* to make each other feel bad? No, the whole point of joking about something negative is to show that we have power over it.

You, my friend, are in control of that blatantly expanding waistline. I promise it's no big deal. Now have a laugh.

In this case, I also wanted to make The Joke because of where we were shooting the special. Not sure if you're aware, but Washington, D.C., is pretty close to another little city called Baltimore. And Baltimore has a bit of what we might call . . . a reputation. It's tough, it's gritty, it's dangerous. It's very used to being considered D.C.'s crime-ridden stepbrother. (*The Wire*, anyone?) I decided to warm up the local crowd by riffing on Baltimore's hard-edged reputation. Again, maybe you didn't like The Joke, and that's fine. But there was no hidden agenda, there was no darker, devious purpose. It was a gag. That's all.

Honestly? My guess is that most of my critics actually know this. Which brings me to WitchTok.

Now, if someone has a genuine problem with my comedy, and they passionately post a message going at me, what can I say—I believe in free speech, and if I believe in it for me, I need to believe in it for you. But the truth is that most of the outrage directed against me and The Joke is not at all sincere. It's not a controversy, it's a nontroversy. And it's manufactured for one reason and one reason alone—to game the algorithm.

If you're trying to rise on TikTok and grow an audience, one guaranteed method is to monitor trends and draft on them for clout. *Oh, Pokémon's big? I'm doing a post on that. The show* Suits *is surging as a topic? I'm a huge fan. Matt Rife said something people are upset about? That's crazy . . . never liked the guy! Now here's my promo code for Casper mattresses.*

As it turns out, just putting "Matt Rife" in any video boosts the signal and helps it go viral. Now don't get me wrong—no one knows better than I do that social media and TikTok specifically helped turbo-boost my career. But it's also true that the same platforms have magnified so-called outrage about my comedy to a deafening level. A blessing and a curse.

How do I know that 99 percent of the fury is bullshit? Because trolls don't just sit around waiting for me to say something they disagree with so they can comment on it—they go through years and years of internet archives to *actively search* for new things to be offended by. This pattern is so common these days that we're all a little desensitized, but let's think about this, okay? If you are so genuinely traumatized by something in the world, *why the fuck* are you spending all your time looking for more of it?

Like, yeah, when my Black buddy and I were roasting each other on Twitter back in junior high, I quoted a famous rap song that used the n-word. I have zero memory of this, but apparently it happened, because someone, somewhere, somehow, unearthed it online.

My response? On the one hand—*man*, I could be a fucking moron. On the other hand—congrats, you have unburied a twenty-year-old text that proves that, like most other adolescents, *man*, I could be a fucking moron. I didn't hide, I didn't apologize— I owned my juvenile mistakes and said my piece, which ended up being the closing bit of *Only Fans* if you need a refresher.

Do you really think I cheer on domestic violence? Do you really think I'm a racist? Do you? Or are you just hunting for more nontroversy so you can feed the beast and get clicks?

I guarantee it's the latter. But I'll be honest. That Sunday morning when the outrage exploded, I didn't exactly feel great about everything. Fuck my popularity—I had enough followers on social to last a lifetime, and drama usually just led to more, as strange as that sounds. That wasn't the problem.

The problem was I'm fucking human—and I actually happen to like other humans. I've dedicated my life to making people laugh. I wanna lift people up and give them joy. I hated the idea that I really had caused anyone to be upset, if they really were. I didn't want to hurt anyone.

Now I had to make a decision. A huge one.

What should I do? Should I publicly apologize to everyone? Even if any harm I had caused was entirely unintentional? And if so, what exactly should I say?

TBH, it wasn't a very hard decision to make.

No one calling for my head wanted a real apology. They wanted the thing that passes for an apology on social media. A generic "To all those I have offended . . ." note. Or worse, the totally staged hostage-video posted to Instagram. You know the one—with the messy hair and the Vicks VapoRub under the eyes, where the chastened celeb sobs about how *they've changed a lot in the last twenty-four hours. Sincerely!*

No one buys those "apologies," and why should they? They're never really for the people who were offended. They're for the celebrity's reputation. They're meant to signal "My bad! Won't happen again!" to any brands who might be getting nervous about their sponsorships. The apologies are for L'Oréal and Bud Light, not for you.

Of course, they make the trolls happy, too, because then they get to rip you for being a pussy, or for not being authentic enough, or for basically anything they can think up to generate more clicks, which is all they really wanted in the first place.

The second a comedian starts apologizing for material, it's over. You're going to spend the rest of your life being a phony whose only goal is being as bland and inoffensive as possible. But I was fortunate. I had spent the last twelve years of my life building my career—and strengthening my identity.

I know who I am and what I stand for. I don't hate people or promote hate, and I don't have to spend a minute proving that.

The following day, I had an idea. Before I could scare myself out of doing it, I opened my Instagram to Stories and typed: "If I've ever offended you by a joke I've told onstage, here's a link to my official apology . . ."

Followed by an embedded web link to an adult special needs helmet.

Boom, bitch. *That's* how I feel about your "outrage."

My audience, of course, loved it! And by "my audience" I mean the women, men, trans, and disabled people from around the globe who continued to pack every performance in the days and weeks following. Just like I thought, I actually gained more followers from it all. Not only because even nontroversies generate momentum on social media, but because there really are a bunch of people out there who are sick of the hypocrisy of cancel culture and who genuinely appreciate a dude who refuses to bow down to the outrage mob.

My industry had my back, too. I started getting calls from other comedians around the country—some of them my friends, some of them my heroes, some I'd never even met before—all telling me to push on. Did they like the joke? Were they even fans of my comedy? Who knows. It was basically irrelevant. What was relevant was that as comics they'd all been there before. They'd all faced setbacks, been attacked or misunderstood. And they'd all made it through, growing even stronger in the process.

And you know what? Even the performative outrage crowd loved my "apology" in their own way. Because now they had *more* to be outraged by. *How dare Matt Rife link to an adult special needs helmet! He promotes domestic violence—and he's ableist! He has zero respect for those with special needs!*

Ha, okay. Eat dicks.

Yet again my amazingly devoted fan base came to my rescue, reposting all the clips of me actually engaging with disabled members of my audience. Talking to them, laughing with them, and—you're goddamn right—roasting them. Because the worst, most truly offensive thing you can do to someone is ignore them. I've always felt that exclusion is the biggest form of discrimination, because people aren't truly different until you treat them differently.

All my critics were having a ball talking *about* disabled people, talking *around* disabled people, *using* disabled people to further their agendas and gain more clicks. But did any of the trolls ever try to actually fucking talk *to* disabled people? Hell no.

I've been blessed with some of the most beautiful, bonding interactions onstage. I've met everybody—and made jokes *about* everybody. And I'll tell you this: it's almost never the person being joked about that actually takes offense and gets angry. Disability doesn't mean "doesn't have a sense of humor." If anything, the disabled people I've met tend to laugh loudest, because laughter is the best coping mechanism for all the shit they have to deal with.

The same weekend I experienced the Lazy Hero at Copper Blues in Phoenix, I met one of the sweetest women—and for once she may not have been older than me. She was seated in the front row, stage left, in a wheelchair, and her brother had given me the heads-up that she was a huge fan. During the show I asked her a little about herself and we had some fun mocking the hell out of each other, but it's what she concluded with that got me. Her eyes welled up with tears and she said, "Thank you for including me."

Thanks to her, I knew exactly how I was gonna close my second special, *Matthew Steven Rife*. I delved into the hardships of the disabled and how much I admired their mental and emotional strength, plus my appreciation for them *rolling* with the punches, and then I honored them in the best way I know how. With a joke.

"That's what you do to vegetables . . . you roast them."

Guess what? She loved that joke, and if you don't, count your blessings and do what she unfortunately can't: Take a hike.

Looking back on it all with the added perspective of, oh, at least a few months—what would I change about my Netflix special?

I don't know, man. Maybe different camera angles and a better edit. Yeah, the nontroversy caused a lot of headaches for my friends, my family, and my creative team. It put my fans in an awkward position where they felt like they had to defend me. But I had so much fun building that show and a lot of people loved it. And I honestly have yet to engage with anyone who was credibly, legitimately hurt by my comedy.

When you're moving at three hundred miles per hour, there are no small accidents. I knew a backlash was coming. I knew it intuitively. A big part of me was dreading it. Things had been going so ridiculously well. Life over the past year had felt too good to be true. I wasn't used to shit going right—I was used to it going wrong.

I was waiting, just waiting, for everything to go to hell.

When it did—and when I found myself still standing at the end of it—it was like I could finally breathe again. It felt like I could finally say, "Phew. Okay, now this is real. I can trust this. Now I can actually experience this."

Since then, in my own way, that's exactly what I've been trying to do. While still, of course, moving at three hundred miles an hour.

18

LOOK OUT FOR SPIDERS

We walk through the halls of the empty house for sale, bickering over the changes we'll make if we decide to pull the trigger on a purchase.

"This old carpet will definitely *have* to go," I say. "It's all flat and smushed."

"Agreed. Maybe something like a nice, plush beige to match the walls."

"Beige!" I say, gagging. "Absolutely not. More like snowy white, really thick and fluffy, like you sink right into it. And we are totally changing these dingy walls."

"With . . . a new shade of beige, I hope?"

"I want the bedroom to be cream and green," I say. "You know green is my favorite color."

"I do. I do."

"Yeah," I say, "that shit'll look Rolex."

Yep, I think, this house is definitely the one. Perfect for me and my boys. You remember them—one being the dude who opens for me on tour to this day, who never ever shuts up, and who obviously is gonna be my roommate in this five-bedroom house I'm gonna buy.

What—did you think I was married or some shit? Hell no! I'm not even thirty yet, who the fuck needs that kind of grief? Besides, Alex and I are already basically married. We just have more sex than the average married couple. Kidding.

Probly the same amount.

"Okay, I know we're buying the place furnished," Alex says as we walk out the front door together, "but I insist on a new couch, and of course we'll need TVs for every room, and Xboxes, and . . ."

I sigh and roll my eyes. I might just have to banish this moth-erfucker to the pool room. Oh, and FYI, buying a furnished house isn't ideal. It feels like you're in an Airbnb that the owners died in.

My house—the first one I've ever owned, and a slight step up from the sofas I'm used to sleeping on—is located between two major cities on the East Coast, and there's a comedy club and air-port not too far away, so it's really convenient for all the touring I do. I'd like to tell you more about the location, but honestly, some fans are so rabid they'd find me and try to eat me alive if I gave out too much information. No joke. I've been bit.

The house is on a bunch of land, too. I don't mean it's some fancy estate or something. I'm talking about nature. Real nature. Like I'm walking around right now, dictating this shit into my phone, and I'm seriously looking at a pair of giant-ass wild turkeys strutting across the yard, along with—

FUCK! SO FUCKING GROSS!—

Okay, I just walked through a spiderweb. Which is the one and only downside of living out in nature, because spiders are the absolute worst. Just creepy and crawly and their stringy-ass webs just stick to you and won't come off. Blech. Disgusting.

It's funny, I guess, because I spent most of the first half of my life trying to get away from the nothing fields of central Ohio. And don't get me wrong, I still can't stand rural white-trash Ohio. But now that I could live in pretty much any huge fancy city in the world, the first thing I wanted to do was move closer to nature.

I'm aware that some people prefer the flashing lights and big buildings and concrete of the cities, some people hate to go camping or sit outside and watch the fireflies light up at dusk, but to me it's so crazy that anyone doesn't like nature. I mean, it's *nature*, it's *natural*, that's where we're supposed to be as human beings. That's where we're from, that's where we'll end up when we're dead and buried, that's what this whole world will be when it finally comes to an end. Nature, just nature.

Don't get me wrong. I don't believe in hippy-dippy bullshit and I will always, *always* draw the line at crystals, but somehow, for some reason, it calms me to stand in my bare feet on the grass or to reach out and touch a stone or whatever it may be. It's good for you.

Though I will say that the very first thing I bought for the house was a Nerf basketball hoop for the entrance. Because blindsiding your boy with a windmill 360 dunk is good for you, too—and for maintaining the pecking order of the foyer.

You know what I mean—the simple stuff.

We're only about 70 percent through the ProbleMATTic World Tour as I finish this book. How I've had the time to write it, I don't know. But I think it was healthy. I haven't had the chance to reflect on much of this journey—the wins, the losses—and it's been a pleasure to share my insane experiences of my past and present. The future is scary, but what's life without a little danger?

I'm gonna be honest with you guys. I love having the opportunity to make so many people laugh. I love getting paid to do it. Who knows where I'll be in twenty years or even twenty weeks, but right now I am truly living my dream, and I will be forever grateful that I finally broke through. Trust me, I know how much luck and hard work it takes to make it happen.

But being famous is fucking weird. There's not much positive about it. From when I was a little kid, I've always had problems trusting people. I mean, you try feeling secure in the world when your dad kills himself, your stepdad abuses you, and even your grandpa, who you love more than anything, pretty much wants to isolate himself from humanity. Maybe Papaw was on to something.

Being famous has magnified all that trust shit by a million. Forget about the trolls—it goes without saying that at this point I get attacked online on the regular by thousands of people who don't even know me. I get that. It comes with the territory. But man, I can't even trust the people who pretend to *like* me. How can I? They all want something from me. And I'm not saying they're all these diabolical, devious motherfuckers sitting around twirling their mustaches and cackling "*Mwahaha!* Now we finally have Matt exactly where we want him!" Shit, if anything, that would be kind of funny. Who doesn't like a fun twirling mustache and a nice cackle? Give 'em a top hat and a Bolshevik accent and we're good to go.

No, a lot of the "nice" people probably think they have my interests at heart. They might truly believe it. But still—they all *want something*. They are only here, they are only talking to me, because after years of working my ass off and getting nowhere, a few turns of fate gave me a level of success that was undeniable. That was impossible for them to not want to be a part of somehow. And trust me, people will turn on you the moment it benefits them.

Go back in time just a few months, and these same people who currently smile and give me Hollywood hugs and tell me how much they love me—they quite literally wouldn't stop on the street if I tried to hand them free tickets. And the same people who "adored me" yesterday are already trying to take everything from me today, the moment I'm not what they want me to be.

How am I supposed to navigate this? You tell me, guys. Because if there's a secret, I seriously want to know.

I'm single right now. Would I like to get married someday? Sure. Have a few kids? Why not. Let's say three—two boys and one girl. No idea why that mix, but it feels like a good combination, so I'm sticking with it. But how exactly am I supposed to meet the right girl?

Let's be clear—I am not stressing over this in any way whatsoever. But think about how hard it is to meet the right person even in the best of scenarios. Someone where you both respect each other and support each other and don't spend all your time arguing about stupid shit. And yeah, someone you can trust. That person is one in a million even when you're *not* famous. What the fuck am I supposed to do now? Go on Plenty of Fish? Slide into someone's DMs on Insta? Who knows—maybe I'll end up with Christina from Des Moines. She's fucking hot, and men from Iowa are clearly blind, so she's probably still available.

Then there's my sleep. As you may have picked up throughout the book, sleep has always been . . . kind of a problem for me. In a way there's nothing complicated about that—it's just insomnia. When some people get stressed and depressed and anxious, they eat too much, they drink too much, they sleep too much. Me? I *don't* sleep. At all. I lie there in my bed, and my mind bounces from one thing to another. Sometimes it's work, sometimes it's the most recent individual who fucked me over, sometimes it's totally random.

Yellow.

Trees.

The circus.

Space.

But a few months ago, in the middle of ProbleMATTic, it was out of control. I was walking to a show in Indiana, I hadn't slept *at all* for seven straight days, and I collapsed.

Grasshoppers.

Computers.

I was forced to do what I hate more than anything—postpone my tour. For two weeks straight I did nothing but try unsuccessfully to get rest and go see doctors who basically couldn't figure out what to do. It started to feel like I was never going to find a solution or sleep ever again.

Snow.

Baseball.

Stop sign.

They were like, "You know how people's circadian rhythms can get off?"

"Sure," I said.

"Well, you don't even *have* a circadian rhythm at all anymore."

Apparently, doing two shows a night almost nonstop for a year and a half on end without ever seeing the light of day isn't, like, good for you. I was only twenty-eight, but I had the fucked-up health and jaded soul of a ninety-year-old. If Grandpa Steve was still with me, I probably would've sold my new house and moved in with him.

Plastic-covered furniture for everyone!

———

I know. Good luck on finding a way to make that any less depressing. Cue the fucking violins, right? But honestly, guys—I'm good. I really am.

At the end of my forced vacation, I finally—finally—was able to get a few hours of sleep, a few days in a row. And then it was back on the road and back onstage, which ironically my body had been craving more than sleep itself. More than anything else, it turns out I can't live without performing. More than anything else, I don't want to disappoint my fans and all the people I love who are relying on me. Those two weeks had felt spiritually like two months.

Comedy is in my blood. Making people laugh is who I am. And that's a good thing. Fuck that—it's a *great* thing.

People in the entertainment business finally seem to take me seriously. Instead of rejecting my ideas out of hand, they're actually inviting me to give pitches in corporate conference rooms to a handful of executives who have no imagination—and *then* they reject my ideas. It's awesome! But I've managed to sneak a few through, and I already have some movies and projects in different stages of production. I'm very hopeful and super excited.

I got all my friends who've been with me since the very beginning, so I *know* I can count on them. I got Alex, who I love, but who'll definitely be living in the pool house at some point. I got Kyle, my buddy and current videographer, who's also moving in. A couple more who pop in sometimes. My best buddy James decided to go off and have himself a kid, which I'll never forgive him for, but I got him, too.

The core of my team and my close comedy community—my manager Christina and friends like Paul, who chose to stick with me even when it would've been easier to sell me out—I will always have their back, because they've always had mine.

Me and my mom are doing better than ever after some rough spots in our relationship. I'm in fucking therapy, y'all. Imagine that—me. In therapy. Yeah, yeah, I know, self-reflective and shit.

Most of all, somewhere out there in the universe, I know I got Papaw. Grandpa Steve is out there looking over me, guiding me, protecting me. Loving me, and probably chewing tobacco and watching raunchy movies, if there's any such thing as heaven. Without him, none of this would be possible. None of it.

I'm doing my best to accept all this—the great, the good, and the not-so-good. It's my dream, absolutely, but it's also a lot of madness to pack into two years. Sometimes I feel like an old man, but in a way I'm still just a kid. I gotta remember that. I gotta be kind to myself. I gotta learn to be patient and more forgiving, of myself and others.

And sometimes, when I need it most, I gotta take time to rest. To shoot a few hoops with my Nerf basketball. To feel the grass on my feet and reach out my hand to touch a stone.

Sorry there weren't more pictures in this book.

ACKNOWLEDGMENTS

Mom: Without your lack of contraception and the love you give me, there'd be no book. No story to tell. No me. And there would be less laughter in the lives of millions and millions of people around the globe who may desperately need it. Thank you for letting me leave the nest to start a life of my own and chase this impossible dream that will change the course of our family name forever. I love you so much.

My sisters: Thank you for being a living testament to all of this. You've been with me since I was five years old. You've seen the traumas and the explosions that have shaped my life, and I'm so grateful to have shared it with you. Seeing you grow into the strong, smart, beautiful mothers you are now, watching you start your families—it's been so inspiring. A true joy to watch. With all the holidays I miss and all the flights I have to catch, just know I always love you and we're never far apart. I wish my own happiness for you a hundred times over.

Acknowledgments

Erik Griffin: Thank you for taking a chance on this pimply kid from Ohio. Your mentorship has blossomed into a full family bond. You're the consistent, reliable older brother–figure in my life, and without you I'd be so lost. You've inspired me, motivated me, pissed me the fuck off, and you've taught me the meaning of tough love. Earning your respect as a man and a comedian is one of my most cherished accomplishments, and I keep working on it every day. Your mom should be proud of the good you've done for another person.

James, Paul, Kyle, Kevin, Jackson, and Alex: You dipshits. You absolute moronic lunatics. You're clinically insane, absurd, repulsive, and nobody should ever have to endure who you are as individuals. Which is why I love you. THANK YOU for sharing this roller coaster with me. You ALL have played a very special part in everything I've built. Without you guys, I couldn't have done this. I don't mean physically—I mean mentally and emotionally. You've pushed me to work harder, and I hope it's inspired you, too. You've made me enjoy so much of this experience at times when I could've given up or let it pass me by without embracing how absolutely magnificent this all is. I'm thankful to share this life with you guys. You're my brothers. No matter when or where you came into my life, just know we've got a long ways to go.

Christina Shams: Thank you for believing in me. Thank you for trusting my ideas, my intuition, my crazy plans, and my dreams.

Acknowledgments

Thank you for always fighting for me and protecting me in this insane business. Ten years after we met, we were brought back together to form the perfect team. Thank you for taking a chance on me, and I'm so happy your gamble paid off—because you deserve it. You work just as hard as I do, and that is *so* rare to find. You're the best manager I've ever had, and the one I always wanted. It's been such an honor to watch you blossom into the boss bitch that you are now, and it's been amazing to go through all of this with you, learning, growing, and building what we've always known to be possible.

Martin Amini: Mi hermano! How crazy is this, bro?! I wanna congratulate you on everything you've built and have on the horizon. Six years ago, you took a chance on me, flew me out to D.C. to sell basically no tickets, and welcomed me to a new city that quickly felt like home. Well, we're finally where we said we wanted to be. We said we were gonna do this. We mapped it all out on drives to shows, in the basements, at the monuments late at night. And we did it. THANK YOU for motivating me. You're the kind of friend a guy needs to push him. I can't stop running, because you're still running. We're side-by-side enjoying the journey and the views together, and I look forward to a lifetime of that, brother. Love ya.

Kevin Bisch: Gaaaht dayum, man! Hahahahaha

Sara: Good idea ;)

Acknowledgments

Dave Chappelle: There's zero-percent chance you'll ever read this, but it felt necessary. I was about nine years old when *The Chappelle Show* came out, and like every person from nine to ninety, my friends and I loved it and would quote it nonstop. And because we'd heard you lived in Yellow Springs, Ohio, just forty-five minutes south of us, we used to fantasize about driving down in hopes of running into you. I didn't know twenty years later that I'd be lucky enough to call you a friend and mentor. You're the epitome of what a comedian can and should be. You've seen the highest highs and lowest lows that this business and profession can offer an artist. Your bravery, your intelligence, your wit, and your humor have saved comedy time and time again. The day *Sticks & Stones* came out on Netflix, I stayed up until three a.m. to watch it the moment it launched. Then I watched it four more times. It was the most perfect special I'd ever seen. I wrote twenty new minutes because I was so inspired. I aspire to your fearlessness and sense of self. Because they unlock the best, rarest gift in life . . . freedom. Thank you for your artistic expression, and for your mounds of advice on how to navigate this treacherous, beautiful road ahead.

My fans: Thank you. You don't need me, but boy, do I need you. Thank you for believing in me, supporting me, and enjoying what I have to offer this world. Whether I've helped you smile on a quick scroll through social media, or helped dig you out of a bad day with a good laugh, I'm just happy to help. No one knows better than me what a privilege it is to do what I do, and I'm forever grateful to you for making my dreams come true. I hope you become everything you want to be in this lifetime. But even if you feel like you don't . . . who fucking cares. Did ya enjoy the journey? Because that's what it's all about. We're only here for so little time, so let's laugh. Laughter is love. Spread it and get as much of it as ya can. Thank you for giving me so much love.